there
QUARRY FOR MIDDLEMARCH

By GEORGE ELIOT

Edited, with an Introduction and Notes, by
ANNA THERESA KITCHEL
SOMETIME HENRY NOBLE MACCRACKEN PROFESSOR
OF ENGLISH LITERATURE AT VASSAR COLLEGE

UNIVERSITY OF CALIFORNIA PRESS
BERKELEY AND LOS ANGELES
CAMBRIDGE UNIVERSITY PRESS · LONDON
1950

UNIVERSITY OF CALIFORNIA PRESS
BERKELEY AND LOS ANGELES
CALIFORNIA

◇

CAMBRIDGE UNIVERSITY PRESS
LONDON, ENGLAND

COPYRIGHT, 1950, BY
THE REGENTS OF THE UNIVERSITY OF CALIFORNIA

Preface

There seems of late to be a quickening of interest in the works of George Eliot, and especially in her novel, *Middlemarch*. The Victorian critics, Leslie Stephen, for example, praised her earlier novels and thought *Middlemarch* heavy and "dull," but the contemporary preoccupation with science and especially with psychology has given us new perspectives, and serious students of George Eliot today see in this later novel her most important achievement. Not only its psychological insight and its tight motivation but also its sociological evidence now give it a predominant place in nineteenth-century fiction; for *Middlemarch* is a study not only of personal but of social psychology. The later chapters show an acute observation of mob psychology when Bulstrode and Lydgate become the targets for the gossip of the various town groups.

Middlemarch is a revelation of the life of a small provincial English town in the period from 1829 to 1832 and a revelation also of the way a writer of 1870 looked at the events and the people of forty years before her own day. The *Quarry* shows us how she prepared herself to understand one special aspect of life in that milieu at that time, for half of its pages are almost entirely given over to notes on medical subjects, with some few showing her efforts to fix exactly the date of the story by tying it to the stages of the First Reform Bill.

But *Middlemarch* is not only a social and psychological study. It is a work of art, and the second half of the notebook has as much interest for the student of fiction as the first, perhaps more. For we see here the struggles of the author to make her structure clear and unified.

Of course, the *Quarry* is only a small part of George Eliot's preparations to write *Middlemarch*. In a sense, her whole previous life went into the undertaking. The place and the people she knew—

Middlemarch is, no doubt, Coventry; Caleb Garth is her father, Robert Evans; Dorothea is perhaps her own idealized self. From her girlhood on, she had been eager to know more about science. This interest became more intense after Lewes, who, under the influence of Herbert Spencer, had taken up the study of biology, turned to physiology and finally to researches into physiological psychology. Much of the scientific and medical knowledge that lies back of the portrait of Lydgate must have been communicated to her by her devoted companion and critic. Lewes knew many medical men and his knowledge of the profession and its problems was ever at her command.

A study of the *Quarry* and its sources leads inevitably to a curiosity about medical lore and medical practice in nineteenth-century England. But a professor of English is hardly equipped to produce a sound study on that subject. I have tried merely to check the source of the notes in the first part and have steered clear of any attempt at exposition of the general problem. The references are for the most part identified, but some I have not been able to locate definitely. Future students will doubtless be able to fill in these gaps.

The small size of this monograph must, to any real student of *Middlemarch,* suggest another omission. I have not tried to show how the information jotted down in the notebook appears in the finished novel. My purpose is to make the *Quarry* available to students who have no access to the manuscript in the Houghton Library. Checking the text of the novel by the notes in the *Quarry* should be a fascinating pursuit for anyone seriously interested in *Middlemarch*. The exercises represented in the second half of the notebook should be even more rewarding to a student of the craft of fiction.

My chief acknowledgments must go to Harvard University, the owner of the *Quarry;* to Mr. K. D. Metcalf, the Librarian of Harvard; and to the curators of the Houghton Library, where the manuscript is housed. Professor Gordon S. Haight of Yale has helped me by his enthusiasm for the enterprise and by practical

Preface

information about details. Mr. W. B. McDaniel, II, Librarian of the College of Physicians in Philadelphia, has looked up several references for me and has given me the privilege of publishing a short article on the *Quarry* and its medical material in *Transactions & Studies of the College of Physicians of Philadelphia*.[1]

Some of my colleagues at Vassar College have encouraged me in this undertaking and the college has made possible this study by allotting two sabbatical leaves, short but profitable, to my use. I am also indebted to the Lucy Maynard Salmon Fund for Research, established at Vassar College in 1926, for a grant to assist in the publication of this *Quarry for Middlemarch*.

ANNA T. KITCHEL

Poughkeepsie, N.Y.,
June, 1949.

---
[1] Fourth series, Vol. XIII (Dec., 1945), pp. 129–133.

Introduction

On June 15, 1923, Quaritch, the dealer in manuscripts and rare books, cabled from London to Miss Amy Lowell a long code list of items with the price of each.[1] The items were to be sold at Sotheby's on June 27. Miss Lowell evidently cabled back on June 15, for on that day Mr. Quaritch sent her a letter in which he gave her his idea of the value of the lots. On June 27, he wrote that he was sending, as a result of her "commission at today's sale at Sotheby's":

	Limit	Bought for
516 Browning	100	45
541 Keats	20	2
561 Stowe	20	8 £ 5/
574 Notebook	100	105

The notebook is entitled "Quarry for Middlemarch" and was left with the rest of Miss Lowell's library to Harvard University at her death in 1925.

The *Quarry* is a small, black leather notebook, 4⅛ by 6½ in. On the cover an undecipherable title in gilt script is concealed by a paper label inscribed in George Eliot's hand, "Quarry for Middlemarch." About half the book is devoted principally to notes on scientific, and especially medical, matters, with three pages, 23, 24, and 26, listing mottoes for chapters, and one, 25, presenting political dates drawn from the *Annual Register*. This first half of the notebook we shall speak of as *Quarry I*. The notebook was then turned over and again almost exactly half of it was used, chiefly for the working out of the structure of the novel, though a few pages are devoted to political dates concerned with the passage of the First Reform Bill. This part of the notebook we shall call *Quarry II*.

---

[1] Cables and letters in the Lowell Collection of the Houghton Library, Harvard University.

Evidence from George Eliot's Journal and letters, which need not be detailed here, indicates, though not conclusively, that the *Quarry* was begun soon after September, 1868, and was used until *Middlemarch* was almost completed. More important than the date is the consideration of the way in which it was used.

With the exception of the three pages devoted to chapter mottoes and the one given up to "Political Dates," *Quarry I* is composed of jottings of informative data which, as George Eliot put it in her Journal, September 21, 1869, were "necessary to my imagining the conditions of my hero." By that date, then, the leading role in the "Vincy and Featherstone parts" had been assigned to the young doctor, Lydgate. These "conditions" needed a basis of plain fact, which her gleanings in medical magazines and books afforded. We shall consider her medical notes shortly, but must ask first, "Why make a doctor the hero of one of the main stories in *Middlemarch?*"

Lydgate is, of course, a creation of the author's imagination, but that imagination almost always worked on remembered reality, and it seems very possible that the memory which started Lydgate into life dealt with a quite recent experience of the author. On July 23, 1868, Lewes and George Eliot returned from a visit to Baden,[2] and, according to Lewes's diary, he went soon afterward to Oxford to a meeting of the British Medical Association. The diary continues, "In September we went to Leeds—guests of Dr. Allbutt (whose acquaintance I began at Oxford) . . ."[3] This may have been the first meeting of the novelist and the Leeds physician, but Allbutt's biographer, Sir H. D. Rolleston, suggests that he and Lewes had begun to know each other some years earlier, before Allbutt went to Leeds.[4] Be that as it may, in September, 1868, Lewes and George Eliot visited Allbutt in Leeds and saw the hospital to which in 1861 he had been elected Physician—"The Leeds House of Re-

---

[2] J. W. Cross, *George Eliot's Life as Related in Her Letters and Journals* (London, 1885), III: 46.

[3] Anna T. Kitchel, *George Lewes and George Eliot* (New York: John Day, 1933), p. 252.

[4] Sir H. D. Rolleston, *Sir Clifford Allbutt: A Memoir* (New York: Macmillan, 1929), p. 14.

Introduction 3

covery, one of the earliest fever hospitals in the country."[5] George Eliot wrote to Barbara Bodichon, September 25, 1868, "Our host, Dr. Allbutt, is a good, clever, graceful man, ... and the fine hospital ... is admirably fitted for its purpose."[6] In a letter of May 26, 1869, she spoke of Dr. Allbutt, "our charming friend at Leeds."[7] He had evidently made a memorable impression on her mind.

Dr. Rolleston was sure that Allbutt suggested to George Eliot some of the characteristics of Lydgate.[8] And in the biography of a greater doctor than either Allbutt or Rolleston may be found a contemporary story that must carry weight. When Sir William Osler was a young man, he spent some time studying in London. He was always an admirer of the portrait of a medical man achieved in the character of Lydgate and has this to say of a memory of his London days which connected with his favorite *Middlemarch:* "It is often said that my Brother Regius of Cambridge, Sir Clifford Allbutt, was the original Lydgate. Nothing in their careers was in common, save the training and the high aspirations. There is a basis for the statement. When Dr. Bastian lived at Hanwell, one Sunday afternoon he had just returned from a visit to George Eliot, and the conversation turned on *Middlemarch* which had recently appeared. He said the matter had been discussed in her house that afternoon, and she confessed that Dr. Allbutt's early career at Leeds had given her suggestions."[9]

Dr. Rolleston notes differences between the circumstances of Dr. Allbutt and Lydgate[10] and quotes a statement of Lewes's to Alexander Main that "George Eliot had no acquaintance in any degree resembling Lydgate." Nevertheless, he, himself, accepts as a fact the great importance of Dr. Allbutt to George Eliot's creation of her medical hero.

---

[5] Rolleston, p. 21.
[6] Cross, III: 52–53.
[7] Cross, III: 76.
[8] Rolleston, pp. 59–62.
[9] Harvey Cushing, *Life of Sir William Osler* (New York: Oxford University Press, 1925), I: 463 n.
[10] Rolleston, p. 60.

Doubtless more than one medical man contributed to that creation. There were at least three practitioners of the medical or surgical art whom George Eliot knew before she met Dr. Allbutt. The first was Edward Clarke, a surgeon practicing in Meriden, who married her sister, Christiana Evans, in 1837. The second was Dr. Bury of Coventry, who cared for Robert Evans in his last illness and who was the father of George Eliot's intimate friend Mrs. Congreve. Dr. Bury was connected with the Coventry and Warwickshire Hospital, one of two surgeons attending that institution.[11] The third acquaintance was Dr. John Chapman, with whom George Eliot was associated while he was editor of the *Westminster Review*. Chapman's career is interestingly described by Professor Gordon Haight in his *George Eliot and John Chapman*. Chapman did not take his medical degree till May 6, 1857, when, remarks Professor Haight, "By hook or by crook, he managed to compress the whole of his medical education into nineteen months."[12] By that time he and his former assistant were seeing little or nothing of each other. His career as a doctor could, I think, have had little influence on her conception of her medical hero in 1868–1869; nor is there any trace of a contribution by the career of her brother-in-law, Edward Clarke. Dr. Bury's experience at the Coventry hospital, however, may have furnished suggestions for Lydgate's problems. In the early 'thirties, I am told by Professor Haight, there was a situation in which the Coventry and Warwickshire Hospital was in competition with a new hospital set up to give cheaper treatment than the old institution afforded. The parallel is not at all clear-cut, but George Eliot surely must have known of this rivalry and may have used the general situation as a background for the rivalry of the Middlemarch Infirmary and the New Fever Hospital.

George Eliot must have known a good many doctors, not only in the usual relationship of patient and medical attendant but also through Lewes's wide acquaintance with medical scientists. Her

---

[11] F. White, *Warwickshire* (London, 1850), pp. 492–493.
[12] Gordon S. Haight, *George Eliot and John Chapman* (New Haven: Yale University Press, 1940), p. 95.

Introduction 5

interest in and admiration for the profession was the result of a whole complex of experience and not attributable to any one or any two or three doctor friends. The personality and early career of Dr. Allbutt seems to me the most probable "germ" of young Lydgate; what makes Lydgate "real" is the deep sympathy and the subtle psychology with which he is depicted.

Lydgate is an individual working in a complex situation, and his appeal to our belief rests on the credibility of the circumstances in which he is placed. In one sense *Middlemarch* is a historical novel, for its author, in order to make her hero believable, must know a fair amount about the problems which he, living forty years before the time at which she was setting down his history, would have to confront in a small provincial town; what he would know; what ideals and hopes he would be apt to cherish; what obstacles and frustrations he would have to face.

One of her first concerns, apparently, was to stress his deep interest in pure science, for on the verso of the flyleaf of her notebook she set down the names of scientists, chiefly of the eighteenth century, but including Paré and Vesalius from the sixteenth. In all probability this list came out of her reading of Renouard and Russell in August and September, 1869. Later notes give better evidence that Lydgate was to be ambitious in scientific research as well as in the practice of medicine.

The first pages of the *Quarry* are covered with notes taken from the London *Lancet,* dealing with a wide variety of subjects. A study of them suggests that the novelist was trying to find out what attitude a young physician of that time (1829–1832) would have been likely to take in connection with the problems that were facing him and his fellow practitioners. "Reform" was the watchword of the time, and the reform movement was invading medical circles as well as the political world. The first note in *Quarry I* has to do with an abortive effort to get a medical man elected Coroner for Middlesex County. The note is chiefly interesting because it introduces us to that stormy petrel of nineteenth-century medical journalism,

6 Introduction

Thomas Wakley. Today we may acquaint ourselves with the whole career of this fighter for reform in the pages of Sir Squire Sprigge's biography of Wakley,[13] and we may find many a parallel between the interests of the editor of the *Lancet* and the notes jotted down in the first pages of *Quarry I*.

Wakley fought the great "Colleges"—the College of Physicians, the College of Surgeons, and the Apothecaries Hall—because of their cramping control not only of medical practice but also of medical education. Notes from the *Lancet* on the latter subject appear in *Quarry I* on pages 2, 4, 6–7. Perhaps the most explicit attack on the Colleges for their attitude to the training of physicians and surgeons appears in a book published in London in 1826, *Exposition of the State of the Medical Profession in the British Dominions*, etc. This particular passage was not noted down in the *Quarry*, but must have been read by George Eliot and probably influenced her idea of what might have been considered the best education for a doctor in the years just before her novel begins. "The course of education... which at present (1826) exists in Edinburgh seems to approach most nearly to perfection in this country."[14] Doubt might be expressed of this "perfection," and, indeed, Professor Haight has shown that some of the training required for a Scottish M.D. was most superficial.[15] But the *Lancet* seems to throw its emphasis on the merits of Edinburgh as against the shortcomings of London, and George Eliot fell in with this view enough to give her doctor-hero part of his education in Edinburgh, as well as part in London and part in Paris. One advantage of Paris for the student of surgery was that bodies for dissection were more easily obtainable there.[16] Another advantage of study in Paris is to be seen in connection with the diagnosis and treatment of fever to be mentioned later.

Medical education is necessarily connected with hospital training, and several notes in *Quarry I* refer to hospitals and dispensaries. On

---

[13] Sir Squire Sprigge, *Thomas Wakley, His Life and Times* (London, 1897).
[14] *Exposition of the State of the Medical Profession in the British Dominions*, etc. (London, 1826), pp. 342–343.
[15] Haight, pp. 93–94.
[16] See *Quarry I*, p. 7.

Introduction 7

pages 7 and 8 we find notes on the discrimination in London hospitals against students from the country and on the refusal of the College of Surgeons to accept certificates from county hospitals: "yet, says Wakley, the county hospitals are better than the London: the men as eminent, the hospitals not so crowded with pupils."[17] Not that George Eliot believed that provincial hospitals approached perfection, for the "Letter on Hospitals" quoted on the first two pages of *Quarry II* noted inadequacies in the hospital situation in her own town of Coventry.

Even if the embryo medics of 1830 could have had better training, other difficulties would have faced them. Doctors, for the most part, expect to earn their living by their profession; the relation of medical practice to economic conditions was important. The question of fees comes up several times in the *Quarry* entries, on page 6, for example. And the obverse of the problem, the difficulty that poor people had in getting good medical treatment, is not omitted. On pages 1 and 7–8, notes from the *Lancet* deal with the spread of self-supporting dispensaries, where poor folk could receive medical attention.

The difficulty the poor had in getting their ailments treated was one cause of the prevalence of quack medicine. But quack doctors found patrons not only among the poor, but among "fine titled people," who, according to a note on page 7 of *Quarry I*, gave "their certificates as eye-witnesses to St. John Long," "noblemen and gentlemen" attesting his extraction of a "fluid like mercury" from the temples of his "patients." The *Exposition* blamed part of the prevalence of quack medicine on the limitation of the number of well-trained medical men brought about by the narrowness of the great and powerful Colleges.

The last note taken from the *Lancet* deals with the cholera epidemic which invaded England in November, 1831. Its spread into Russia had already been noted on page 4.

Lydgate was a member of a professional group and would be

---
[17] See *Quarry I*, p. 8.

interested in all the general problems confronting the profession. He was also an individual practitioner, caring for individual patients. A few of his "cases" play important parts in his career as a medical man; Fred Vincy's typhoid fever, Mr. Casaubon's heart disease, Raffles's delirium tremens, all enter crucially into the story of the young doctor's *Middlemarch* life. Less important are Mr. Borthrop Trumbull's pneumonia and Nancy Nash's cramps brought on by a starvation diet, but these, too, show Lydgate's skill and honesty and rouse the jealousy of the other practitioners and even of one of the "physicians" of the town.

George Eliot's notebook shows some of the reading through which she prepared herself to deal realistically with the three "important" cases. At the bottom of the second page in *Quarry I* we find a brief item: "Elliotson on diseases of the Heart reviewed. Laennec's discoveries as to the symptoms." No notes from Elliotson appear, but it is very probable that the novelist read either his book or the original lectures on which it was based. The lectures had appeared in the *Lancet* in 1829. Lydgate says that Casaubon is suffering from "fatty degeneration of the heart," a once common but now outlawed term which Elliotson did not use in his lectures but did use in a later book, *The Principles and Practice of Medicine,* the first American and second London edition of which was published in 1844. Whether the now taboo term was suggested by Elliotson it would be hard to prove, for it was common enough even by the time George Eliot was writing of Casaubon's heart disease. In the original lectures the treatment of what is there called "hypertrophy of the heart" included venesection (bleeding), the use of cathartics, digitalis, and other drugs, insistence on a low diet, rest, and the avoidance of all excitement."[18] The omission of bleeding from Lydgate's treatment is worth noting; George Eliot, perhaps, wished to show him as a man ahead of his time.

Casaubon's is not the earliest case in which we see Lydgate at work. We meet him first as old Mr. Featherstone's attendant, but

---

[18] *Lancet*, Oct. 24, 1829, pp. 142–144.

first see him really in action taking care of Fred Vincy's typhoid fever. The fever does not prove as fatal to Fred as it does to his doctor, who becomes intimate with Fred's sister Rosamond and finally marries her. The first practitioner called in by the Vincys did not take Fred's ailment very seriously, but Lydgate has had the training which makes him able to diagnose the trouble correctly. On pages 16-19 of *Quarry I*, after a summary, "Distinction of Typhus and Typhoid Fevers," we find a series of notes on the "Treatment of Fever" as recommended by Dr. Watson. War conditions have made it impossible to consult the first English edition of the book from which these notes were taken, but they check very well with the American edition of 1844. (See *Quarry I*, notes 66-75.) The advertisement of the book, dated 1843, states that it was compiled from lectures given at the Medical Session of 1836-1837 and first printed in the *Medical Gazette*. The distinction between typhus and typhoid fever was still a matter of violent discussion in Great Britain in 1830, and Dr. Watson is not very clear concerning the difference although he acknowledges the importance of ulceration in the glands of Peyer in the fever now called typhoid. George Eliot's notes are clearer on the distinction between the fevers than are Dr. Watson's statements, for by 1870 the old controversy had been laid to rest. Lydgate's reading of "Louis' new book on Fever"[19] again puts him into the class of practitioners ahead of the general run and shows the value to him of his Paris experience.

The third of Lydgate's important cases is Raffles's delirium tremens, out of which develops the public clamor over Bulstrode's and Lydgate's connection with Raffles's death. In *Quarry I* the last lines of page 29 and all the notes on pages 30-31 are devoted to items taken from a small book or pamphlet published in Boston in 1831, "Remarks on the History & Treatment of Delirium Tremens, by John Ware, M.D." It would be interesting to discover how George Eliot got on the track of this pamphlet. It gave her a chance to show once more Lydgate's courage in using methods not popular

---
[19] *Middlemarch* (London, 1885), I: 248.

with his fellow practitioners in England. That theories like Dr. Ware's had met with some attention in England is shown by a report in the *Lancet* from the Middlesex Hospital of four cases of delirium tremens, in three of which opium and stimulants failed. "This circumstance affords some ground for calling in question the propriety of adhering always to that plan of treatment."[20] We have no way of knowing whether George Eliot pursued her *Lancet* reading into the numbers for 1833. Those that she did read, 1830 through March, 1831, contained one review that showed the current practice in treating Raffles's disease. The book reviewed was "A Practical Essay on the Disease generally known under the denomination of Delirium Tremens, etc. by A. Blake, M.D., etc., London, 1830." The reviewer remarks, "His method can differ but little from that generally acknowledged as most efficacious, i.e. a cautious and moderate employment of stimulants and opium (more opium in the second stage of delirium)."[21] More violent administering of opium is recommended in the report of a case by James Whitaker, who asserts that "it is safe to give opium regardless of quantity till a decided effect is produced."[22]

The difference between Dr. Ware's method of treating delirium tremens, which Lydgate decided to follow, and the current English practice raises a nice point in Lydgate's psychology. He cannot help suspecting that Bulstrode, by departing from his instructions to keep both liquor and opium away from Raffles except for very small doses, has been responsible for the patient's death. Yet what good would it do to accuse the banker, since any jury of English doctors would consider him justified? Bulstrode's change of heart concerning the loan which Lydgate had requested makes Lydgate suspicious, and when the banker's reasons for fearing Raffles are revealed, Lydgate is overcome by the conviction that he was right: Bulstrode was guilty and he himself, because he had not accused him, must go down to ruin.

[20] *Lancet*, Oct. 26, 1833, p. 172.
[21] *Lancet*, June 19, 1830, p. 461.
[22] *Lancet*, June 30, 1832, p. 392.

Introduction 11

George Eliot's *Quarry* notes, then, show some of the sources of her information on the general state of the medical profession in 1830 and on the knowledge and treatment of specific diseases at that time. But Lydgate had other ambitions than to be a member of the progressive element in the medical profession and a conscientious practitioner caring for individual cases. "Lydgate was ambitious above all to contribute towards enlarging the scientific, rational basis of his profession."[23] He was interested especially in Bichat's work on the tissues of the body and wished to follow out some of the sequences of that work. "It was open to another mind to say, have not these structures some common basis from which they have all started, as your sarcanet, gauze, net, satin, and velvet from the raw cocoon? ... What was the primitive tissue?"[24] So Lydgate muses and counts on making some discoveries by the use "not only of the scalpel, but of the microscope, which research had begun to use again with new enthusiasm of reliance."[25]

Page 9 of *Quarry I* gives a list headed "Microscopic Discovery," with a subheading, "Cell-Theory." This list names the important users of the microscope from Leeuwenhoek to Ehrenberg. The name of Robert Brown appears on page 10 and finds its place in the novel when Lydgate offers "Robert Brown's new thing— 'Miscroscopic Observations on the Pollen of Plants' " to Mr. Farebrother in exchange for a specimen that Lydgate coveted.[26] Page 20 of *Quarry I* presents a quotation from an article by T. H. Huxley. (See *Quarry I*, note 76.) It deals with the work of Bichat, which, as we have noted above, Lydgate thought of as worth following. The theory of a "primitive tissue" appears in the quotation on pages 21 and 22 from Raspail's *Nouveau système de chimie organique fondé sur des nouvelles méthodes d'observation*, etc. (see *Quarry I*, note 77). Raspail's name is mentioned in chapter 45 of *Middlemarch*, that chapter so rich in scientific, and especially medical, material.

[23] *Middlemarch*, I: 223.
[24] *Middlemarch*, I: 224, 225.
[25] *Middlemarch*, I: 225.
[26] *Middlemarch*, I: 264.

After two pages, 23–24, taken up by jottings of possible mottoes, some of which were used, some not, we find two pages of miscellaneous material, ranging from notes on Mr. O'Connell's radical political moves through some on the abolition in 1832 of capital punishment of sheep stealing, on "Peruvian bark," on tithes, on the uses of manganese. The notes on pages 28–29 of *Quarry I* are taken from the *Annual Register* and summarize the course of the cholera epidemic in the British Isles, that national catastrophe which looms in the background of *Middlemarch* though its ravages touch no person in the novel.

Thus having filled the first half of her notebook with jottings on her reading in medical treatises, George Eliot turned the book over and used the second half of it for very different purposes. Some of the first pages do indeed offer factual data, but these, with the exception of the "Notes from a letter on Hospitals," on pages 1 and 2, had nothing to do with medical information, but were used to clear up the author's understanding of (1) contemporary events, (2) the topography of her imagined locality, (3) details of the times when certain imagined events occurred, and (4) the relationship between the characters of the book.

The dates of important happenings in the years 1830–1833 appear on the verso of the second flyleaf, with some additions on the other side of the page. They deal chiefly with the course of the First Reform Bill and with the progress of the cholera epidemic which she had already dealt with in Part I of the *Quarry*. The various stages of the Reform Bill served to make exact and explicit the times when various events in the novel occurred, though the historical references are woven in so skillfully that a casual reader scarcely notices them. The chief stages of the cholera epidemic appear here in their chronological order, as a part, that is, of contemporary history and not for their medical significance.

Page 1 of *Quarry II* shows a list of the dates of university examinations at Oxford and Cambridge. These could have been useful only to give the author a clear idea of when Fred Vincy could have taken

Introduction

his examinations for his degree. This is a point so little stressed in the book that the setting down of specific information about it serves to emphasize George Eliot's passion for exactness on even the smallest event in her book. The rest of page 1 and part of page 2 are occupied by the letter from Mrs. Congreve about the Coventry Hospital. Below the letter, page 2 carries notes which serve to clarify in exact fashion what we may call "fictional facts." We find first a list of the directors of the Middlemarch Infirmary, with their occupations and their votes for Chaplain noted. The notetaker's desire to be explicit about geography is illustrated at the bottom of the page, where we find a carefully drawn little map showing the town and the parish centers near by. Lowick, Tipton Grange, and Freshitt all appear, complete with mileage from this place to that, though it must be said that the scale is not very exact. Page 3 deals with what is the very heart of the book, the relations between the characters. But the eleven items are mere jottings, with no indication of what the relations were to be. Page 4 offers another exercise in exactitude; here she sets down the year, and usually the month, of many important happenings in the story.

So far, the notebook entries deal with facts, real facts that lie behind the imaginary history, or imagined facts that were to make the history real. But beginning with page 5 we find a different type of entry. No published form of *Middlemarch,* as far as I know, gives title headings for the chapters, but here in the notebook they are all set down. George Eliot gives the number of pages in each chapter in Parts I and II. Then her zeal for paging flags; the chapters of Part III are not paged at all, those of Part IV are partly paged, page numbers being assigned to chapters 37 to 40 only. Again, the numbers of pages in the chapters of Parts V and VI are entirely omitted, but in Part VII she sets them down for the first six chapters and stops there. In Part VIII, the last section, she gives no page numbers for the first eight chapters, but does give them for all the rest except the last chapter. Why does she put down any of these numbers? And if some chapters are paged, why not all? The answer to the first question is probably to be found in the fact that *Middlemarch* was published as a serial. The parts were to come out every other month, beginning with December, 1871, and the month of publication is given after the title of each part, e.g., "Part I. Miss Brooke. Decr." George Eliot had to shape the material of each part so that it would be suitable for a monthly issue; it must be not too long, not too short. The statement of the number of pages in a chapter would be the result of a careful calculation to satisfy the publisher's demand. As for her omission of the numbers, who can say? We have to keep in mind that the *Quarry* is a private notebook, a laboratory document not meant for show. It presents many problems that tantalize the curious student, problems that, as we first meet them, we can only speculate about, not solve.

The chief interest of these outlines of the eight "Parts" of *Middlemarch* is that they show the novelist as architect. With such a mass of heterogeneous material as she had in hand, each part of the building had to be planned (1) to do its own work and (2) to fit in with the rest of the structure. For example, chapters 11 and 12 are first listed in Part I, then transferred (with changed chapter headings) to Part II. Yet, when Part I was published, the chapters in question had been put back into it. Why, since Part I is entitled "Miss Brooke," should Lydgate and Fred Vincy and his sister be introduced into it? Perhaps the bulk of the first issue would have been too small without these chapters, but I think there was a weightier reason than that for including this material in the first issue. Miss Brooke is a most important person in the novel, but Lydgate is almost, if not quite, as important, and Rosamond and Fred, the whole Vincy family in fact, were important too. It is the *town* of Middlemarch that gives its title to the book; George Eliot is presenting a picture of life in a small, provincial city and wishes her readers to get in the very first monthly part of her novel a glimpse of the townspeople who are to play such influential parts in the drama. Lydgate has been mentioned in chapter 10, and as we read the novel and note the author's intense interest in her young

Introduction

doctor-hero we can see why she wanted him to appear early. But why Fred? The story of his troubles, his debts, and his love for Mary could have waited till Part II. But that would have denied the very thing George Eliot was bound to stress, the importance of the unimportant, the relation of comparatively trivial people to the lives of the chief actors in her drama of life as it really is.

Fred Vincy gave her more trouble, apparently, than almost any other character in the book, if the *Quarry* is worth-while evidence. Chapters 19–21 were first listed in Part II, but were then transferred to Part III, whose opening chapters they formed. They fit in better there, for the main purpose of Part III is to show just how Lydgate became acquainted with Fred's sister, Rosamond. The weaving in of Fred's story required much planning and changing about, but the final result seems to prove the value of the weaver's painful care.

On page 9 of Part II of the *Quarry* we are introduced to what seems to have been one of the author's most absorbing efforts to straighten out in her own mind the relation of events and of characters. Here appears the first of her "lists," entitled "Motives," but it is difficult to see any difference in the kind of items called "Motives" here and called "Elements" on page 24. "Elements" is a less specific word than "Motives," and therefore, perhaps, a better caption for one of these working lists. On page 38, "Course of part VII" is necessarily more specific, since the list deals with the problem of a single "Part" of the book. Page 39 exposes one of the author's Motive-Element efforts under the caption "Conditions," but on page 40 the struggle for a proper list heading is given up entirely and important points in the closing chapters are set down (with a sporadic attempt at numbering them) without any caption at all.

Page 16 presents, again, proof of how George Eliot pinned down her imaginary people by exact data. Here the ages of all the Garth children are given first, and then we are told exactly how old are Bulstrode, Raffles, Joshua Rigg, and even his mother, who never appears in the story at all.

Among the most revealing sections of *Quarry II* are pages 17–22, devoted to the story of Bulstrode before he came on the Middlemarch scene. We get his early history, his marriage to the widow of his employer, the efforts of his wife to find her lost daughter, Sarah Yorke (the name is changed to "Dunkirk" in the published text), the frustrating of these efforts by Bulstrode, who bribes an employee of the Yorke firm to keep secret his chance discovery of Sarah and her husband and child. That child of Sarah Yorke is Will Ladislaw, and his father was the son of Casaubon's Aunt Julia. The secret of Raffles's hold over Bulstrode is revealed. All this lies back of the closing Parts of the novel and comes out in the sensational drama which ruins Bulstrode, and Lydgate along with him.

On page 25 of *Quarry II,* George Eliot interrupts the succession of Motive-Element lists to give a narrative of the steps preliminary to the introduction of a Reform Bill by the Whig party up to the dissolution of Parliament on April 22, 1831. This item connects with that marked 4 on page 24, "Leading up to Mr. Brooke's nomination in April or May 1831," and its appendix, "his failure and loss of appetite for a public career."

Then, on page 26, "Elements of B. VI" are detailed, concerned mostly with the related activities of Will, Dorothea, Lydgate, and Rosamond. But at the end of the list Fred Vincy is to the fore again, "choosing his career" this time. (See *Quarry II,* p. 13.) George Eliot is determined to preserve the integrity of the Fred-Mary story, for it is a necessary part of the book she meant *Middlemarch* to be. This determination immensely complicated the problem of the novel's structure, for the Fred-Mary story stubbornly resisted, apparently, connection with the Dorothea and Lydgate stories, which came together so naturally.

Page 27, "Will Ladislaw & Dorothea," and page 28, "Bulstrode & Raffles," carry out a first, or at least an early, development of Books VII and VIII. Page 29, entitled "Scenes," works out the problems from the dramatic point of view. The expository tendency so strong in the author breaks through, however, and interferes with the suit-

Introduction

ability of the name "Scenes" for the material on page 29. But George Eliot struggles hard to make drama out of her material and succeeds better with her second list of "Scenes" on page 30, though even here some of the items are too much condensed in form to make them deserve the title "Scenes." Pages 29 and 30 should be compared with the outlines of Parts VII and VIII on pages 14 and 15; the "Scenes" are developed with much more psychological and dramatic detail, the order of events is altered—the final form as printed in the published text is very near.

The demands of serial publication forced a careful consideration of the way the parts were to end. On page 31 we find the first notes dealing with this problem, though it must have been in the author's mind from the beginning. The statements here given differ greatly from the endings of Books VI and VII as they were published. Will's departure (end of Book VI) is dramatically presented, not narrated by the Farebrother family. Book VII ends with the scene of Bulstrode's disgrace, followed by a short scene in which Dorothea declares her faith in Lydgate.

Sharing page 31 with this discussion of the endings of the last three parts is a list of the "Remaining Scenes of Part VI." As a matter of fact, most of that part is outlined here. The final item, "Will gone away," was discarded when the scene suggested in item 7 had developed itself in the author's mind.

Since she devoted the next page in her notebook, page 32, to what she called "Sketch 2," it would appear that George Eliot planned to deal with Will's situation at this time in a separate little story as she had dealt earlier with Bulstrode's past. But she fails to make anything consistent of Will's story. Dorothea's sympathy for Lydgate is uppermost in the mind of the author; Will is a part of their drama, and his dilemma demands a dramatic, not a narrative, form. These last pages of *Quarry II* portray George Eliot's efforts to get her actual story clear and, by stating the situations over and over as seen from different angles, to fuse the complex and interdependent elements into a real whole.

On page 33 we are given details about the bursting of the storm on the heads of Bulstrode and Lydgate, and this material is continued on page 34 after "Sketch 2" is concluded. The items are bare jottings, exceedingly condensed. On pages 35 and 36, however, they are taken up with a good deal of detail, many of them in narrative form. The plot of the Raffles story is working itself out. It was a kind of story foreign to George Eliot's experience and unsuited in its sensational, mystery-story nature to her taste as a novelist. Yet the melodramatic quality of the story is relieved of its cheapness by the deep psychological study of Bulstrode's character and of Lydgate's part honest, part rationalized, attitude to the banker's change of heart about the loan. And it is interesting to see how neatly she used the controversial point presented by the difference between the treatment of delirium tremens preferred by most English medical men of the time and that which Lydgate, following the American Dr. Ware, was applying in Raffles's case.

The material treated on page 33 is taken up again in "Conclusion of Part VII" on page 37. The items are still mere jottings, with little added except a question at the end about the connection of Will's return. Will's comings and goings are somewhat hard to follow in the finished novel. We note that the author, too, had her troubles with that young man's here-again, gone-again habits.

After a straightforward, itemized account of the "Course of Part VII" on page 38, we find, on page 39, the author considering again the question of Will's return, its reasons, its timing. There follow other questions which she wishes to answer in her own mind: What will happen to Stone Court? How do Fred and Mary fare? What happens "about Dorothea's money, over and above her own 700 a year"? All these items are included under one of the familiar list headings, "Conditions." Below them on the same page, under the caption "Times," we find the specific dating of (1) the death of Raffles, (2) Bambridge's return, and (3) the meeting on sanitary reform. The last item, "Return of Will Ladislaw," is undated.

A sporadic jotting down of points under the title "Part VIII"

Introduction

begins on page 40. There is a combination of mere items, "1 Dorothea & Lydgate" for example, and narrative summaries, as in the point numbered 3. Page 41 has on it only one line, "Dorothea's motive in going to Rosamond."

Page 42, the last in *Quarry II*, presents twelve items, all numbered, which give in clear form the development of Part VIII. A comparison of this page with page 15 shows how much the last section of the novel has been enriched.

Is there any method to be seen in Part II of *Quarry for Middlemarch?* It seems to be: outline, elaborate; outline, analyze, over and over. Beginning on page 5 and continuing through page 15, George Eliot summarized and numbered the chapters of the eight parts, interpolating from time to time lists of points that she had to work out in detail. These lists grow more and more complicated, and the handwriting, usually so fine and clear, grows more careless as she makes progress toward her "Finale."

The *Quarry* shows us clearly what parts of her novel gave her trouble. As the complications increase, as the characters develop, the problem of clarity presses harder and harder. Every motive, every relationship, must be developed until the reader—the careful reader—cannot miss them. The heterogeneous elements of the large and complicated story that made up the novel George Eliot imagined had to be fused into unity. The story then had to be developed with clarity and power.

It is this process of clarification and of fusion that we see working itself out in this small, private notebook which its owner called *Quarry for Middlemarch.*

Quarry One

[Flyleaf, recto]
Quarry for "Middlemarch"
George Eliot
[Flyleaf, verso]

Vicq-d'Azir, b. 1748 ... d. 1794
Pinel, b. 1745, d. 1826   Haller died, 1777
Buffon, 3 first vols. 1749   Linneus at Paris, 1738
Bichat, born 1771, d. 1802   Galvani, d. 1798
Virey, born 1775, died 1840   Jussieu, d. 1831
Laennec, First Memoir on Auscultation, 1818
Broussais, 1772–1838   Brown d. 1788
Ambroise Paré, 1562 ecrivait
Vesalius, born 1513 or 14, died, 1564[1]

(1)

Lancet: 1830. Jan.
Triumph expressed in the Lancet at the great majority for the medical candidate for the office of Coroner of Middlesex in opposition to the attorney—"a medical office, only to be adequately occupied by a medical judge."[2]

Medical Reform at Paris: committee to inquire into the present state of the Hospitals, election of medical officers, public lecturers etc. Members of the Committee, M. M. Cuvier, Dubois, Duméril, etc.[3]

Foundation of the association called "Metropolitan Society of General Practitioners in Medicine, etc.[4]
Professional remuneration. Decision of Ld. Tenterden in the cause of Handey vs. Henson, 1829.* (Assn. dissolved, 31[5]

A letter from Derby, speaks of a self-supporting Dispensary "now getting up" where patients are to be doctored for a penny per week. Midwifery 7s. paid 2 months in advance.[6]

Death of Huskisson: his treatment criticized.[7]

---

* Verdict in favor of the right of a general practitioner to charge for his services.
[1] For numbered notes to *Quarry I* see pages 37–41 below.

(2)

Lancet, 1830
"Diary of a Physician" being published in Blackwood[8]

A writer against the College of Surgeons "fearlessly asserts that my professional education has been such as few men have been fortunate enough to enjoy . . . after having studied in the London schools of anatomy, surgery & medicine; attended as pupil & house-surgeon for two years in one of the London Hospitals; passed my examinations, & received my diploma from the College, I spent three sessions in Edinburgh, studying medicine, & one anatomical season in Dublin, & have since visited Paris:"[9]

at an inquest, giving evidence, Mr. G. Taylor, of Kingston, surgeon & M.D.[10]

Elliotson on diseases of the Heart reviewed. Laennec's discoveries as to the symptoms.[11]

Quoted from Hone's Table Book that the Empiric,

(3)

Dr Graham who appeared in London 1782 had a celestial bed, the charge for sleeping in which was £100. Several persons of high rank acceded to his terms, he pretending that it wrought miraculous effects.[12]

Medical jurisprudence, divided into medical police & Forensic Medicine. The Court of Examiners of the Company of Apothecaries have just added this subject to the curriculum.[13]

Willcocks' "Laws relating to the Medical Prof.
"Medical Law now the universal topic."[14]

A treatise on Poisons in relation to Med. Jurisprudence, by Dr Christison, Edinburgh.[15]

"From the reign of Henry VIII to Geo. IV there is neither a charter nor an act of Parlt. on the subject of Medical Polity, which would not disgrace the lowest mechanics' club."[16]

(4)

Cholera in Russia. Oct. 1830.[17]

"What are the privileges of which they (the Coll. of Physicians) can boast? That of demanding by virtue of their "charter" that no physician, if he be not a graduate of Oxford or Cambridge, shall practise in London without one of their licenses" . . . "We had well nigh forgotten another privilege & the by-law which concedes it is entirely, exclusively of their own manufacture. It is that every "fellow" of the college who shall meet in consultation any physician who may not be recognized by the charter & by-laws of the college, shall forfeit, for each offence, five pounds. This by-law applies, amongst others, to the graduates of the University of Edinburgh.[18]

"The diploma of the College of Surgeons," writes one costs 20 guineas & is of no value to the purchaser.[19]

(5)

Hôtel Dieu, Dupuytren, head surgeon: in the midst of the fighting, Nov. 1830.[20]

The decision of the house of Lords on the appeal case of Rose & Searle, conferred upon apothecaries the privilege of prescribing as well as of compounding; & the Apothecaries' Act of 1815, not only confirmed that privilege, but excluded the physician from any such advantage.[21]

St John Long, the quack & his trial, in question Nov, 1830[22]
Duke of Sussex, pres. of Royal Society (against Herschel)[23]

At a meeting of Derbyshire Medical & Surgical Society 10 Dec. 1830, a resolution passed that to charge less than 10/6 in midwifery cases is a "gross violation of the rules of the profession": members pledge themselves to meet no such violator, or any medical man who may have consented to meet him—except in their official situations as officers of the dispensary.[24]

(6)

Practitioners' Remuneration. Dec. 1830

A letter from Manchester proposes a scale of fees for visits, according to three grades of ability to pay in the patients. Complains that "some practitioners in this town are so dastardly in their conduct, as by sneaking, charging every patient, rich & poor alike, one shilling per visit only, & receiving those fees in weekly installments of 3d & 6d, to undersell and undermine the respectable practitioner etc.[25]

The Lancet writes about the theological prejudices against medical studies.[26]

A book on Adulteration & Slow Poisoning: or Disease & death in the Pot & the Bottle, just published. False alarms of the uninstructed on hearing that their porter is mixed with Quassia! their cheese coloured with anatto! their port wine roughened with tannin![27]

School of Edinburgh supplies the great mass of practical

(7)

physicians to England & Ireland.[28]

The Lancet protests against fixed scales of fees as futile, & injurious to young practitioners.[29]

"No hope of promotion in the hospitals to students in the country"—all done by Nepotism. The dons, Sir W. Halford, & Sir Astley Cooper.[30]

In 1823, bodies for dissection hardly to be obtained in London at any price "from the resurrection men." Court of Examiners would not accept certificates of dissections made in Paris, where bodies were plentiful.[31]

Fine, titled people giving their certificates as eye-witnesses to St. John Long. "Noblemen & gentlemen" attesting his extraction of a "fluid like mercury" from the temple.[32]

Proposal to establish a dispensary at Nottingham. Mr. W., cotton spinner, opposing the nomina-

Quarry I

(8)

tion of medical men on the committee. Lancet disapproves the Dispensary. Why should medical men always be expected to do so much work for nothing?[33]

1831

"Parishes usually send their own contracting medical pauper attendant"—who it is well known, frequently contracts at a very low salary.[34]

Meeting to advocate New College of Medicine.[35]
Certificates from County Hospitals not accepted by Coll. of Surgeons: yet says Wakley the county hospitals are better than the London: the men as eminent, the hospitals not so crowded with pupils.[36]

Cholera. About the end of March, 1832, there had been 1530 cases in London, deaths 802.
Quarantine to guard against it in England, June 13, 1831.
First cases occur at Sunderland Nov. 4. Appears at Rotherhithe, Feb. 10, 1832. Again, Sept. Thanksgiving for its departure, Ap. 14, 1833.[37]

(9)
Microscopic Discovery
Cell-Theory

Untersuchungen über Phytogenesis, by Schleiden, 1837
Mikroscopische Untersuchungen. By Schwann, 1838-9
Malpighi, b. 1628 Discovered the capillary blood vessels: structure of skin, Rete Malpighii: air-vessels & nervous system of insects. Applied the microscope to embryology
Leeuwenhoek, b. 1632, gained a livelihood & his first celebrity as a glass polisher, his lenses being the best then made[38]
Contemp'y. Swammerdamm, "l'auteur le plus étonnant sur toute l'anatomie des petits animaux," says Cuvier.
Lyonnet, anatomy of the caterpillar.
Hewson: his description of the blood-discs leaves little even for moderns to improve[39]

Gleichen, precursor of Ehrenberg, invented the method of injection by feeding animalcules on coloured substances.⁴⁰

Period between Leeuwenhoek & Ehrenberg singularly barren. Ehrenberg born 1795. Made a voyage to the east & in 1828–32 published a celebrated description of animals of N. Africa & W. Asia. His great

(10)

work on the Infusoria, in 1838. Inspired by reading, before setting out on a scientific journey in 1829, Robert Brown's just published "Brief account of microscopical observations on the particles contained in the pollen of plants, & on the general existence of active molecules in Organic & Inorganic bodies.⁴¹

An Exposition of the state of the Medical Profession in the British Dominions, & of the injurious effects of the monopoly by usurpation of the Royal Coll. of Phys. 1826.⁴²

1519 College of Phys. instituted. No man to practise physic in or within seven miles of London unless by them allowed. Physicians in other places, not of the Universities, to be examined by them. £5 a month penalty for practising without admission.⁴³

1540. Physicians in London were exempted from certain offices [*written in above:* services], authorized to search apothecaries' drugs & stuffs, & to *practise* surgery. In the same year Barbers forbidden to exercise surgery except in drawing teeth.⁴⁴

(11)

By 34–35 Henry VIII, any person, being no *common* surgeon, may minister outward medicine. It shall be lawful for any person to cure outward sores, notwithstanding the statute of Henry VIII by which the Bishop's License was required for the practice of medicine or surgery.⁴⁵

(By the original statute the College of Physicians consisted of six physicians mentioned by name, & all other persons of the same faculty within the city of London & seven miles without. There was to be elected a President, 4 Supervisors, afterwards called censors, & eight elects.)⁴⁶

Quarry I

By the charter of James I, power was granted to the College to sue for penalties; to retain them for their own use; to examine & correct physicians, apothecaries, & their medicines, & to punish them by fine, imprisonment, & otherwise ... to fine, & imprison such as practise without a license; to examine witnesses, & administer oaths; to search & destroy the drugs of apoths, & to make by-laws.[47]

(12)

By the Charter of Charles II the college is called, President, *Fellowes*, & commonalty, the second term being added. The first 40 Fellows were nominated by the King in the body of the grant. As vacancies might happen, they were to be filled up out of "the commonalty or members"; but *not out of graduates of Oxford or Cambridge more than other members*.[48] ... All fines, after deducting charges, to go to the poor of the parish. (Never complied with.)[49]

Curious to observe, on the one hand, the College of Physicians procuring a law enabling them to prohibit surgeons from practising physic, & on the other, a law authorizing themselves to practise surgery.[50]

In 1556, the College constituted several visitors, throughout the country, with authority not to suffer any to practise but graduates of Oxford or Cambridge, or persons licensed by themselves. All others were to enter into

(13)

recognizance, that they would not practise until they had been examined & approved; & such as refused obedience were to be imprisoned.

But as the interests of the monopoly were not so much concerned in the country, the persecutions of the College were not so well sustained, & in time they fell into disuse.[51]

"The college cannot confer the title of doctor" (apparently the title could only be given by Universities).[52] "Graduates of Ox-

ford & Cambridge deemed by the college entitled to the exclusive privilege of the fellowship."[53]
Licentiates in a state of warfare with the college as being denied their rights of voting etc.[54] Originally no such distinction as that between Fellows & licentiates.[55]

Monopoly of the Fellowship (for gr. of Oxf. & Cam.) "It is notorious that until the middle of the last

(14)

century the persecutions of the College were as bitter against the graduates of Oxford & Cambridge as of any other universities."[56] Not till 1752, that a statute absolutely excluding from the fellowship all but the graduates of the English universities was enacted.[57] "When the choice was between the prolific & cheap seminaries of Scotland & of Leyden on the one hand, & the expensive ones of Oxford & Cambridge on the other, *in each of which not above one student graduated annually*, there was no room for hesitation. The sole object having been monopoly, the statute must be admitted to have been judiciously framed, which while it embraced only the few straggling pupils of Cam & Isis, carefully excluded the many graduates emanating from the metropolis of Scotland, which had then already attained a very high degree of celebrity"...[58]

"Not anywhere seminaries of education in which opportunities of obtaining medical

(15)

instruction are more scanty than in the two English universities; & that they are especially deficient in anatomical & clinical instruction."[59]

The college of Surgeons just as restrictive as the Coll. of Phys. March, 1824, the Court of Examiners decreed that the only schools of surgery they would recognize should be London, Dublin, Edinburgh, Glasgow & Aberdeen: "that certificates of attendance at lectures on anatomy, physiology, the theory & practice of surgery, & of the performance of dissections, be not received except from the appointed professors of anatomy &

surgery in these above named universities; or from persons teaching in a school acknowledged by the medical establishment of one of the recognized hospitals, or from persons being physicians or surgeons to any of those hospitals."—This of course repressed the salutary competition of private with endowed teachers.[60]

(16)

Inefficiency, nay arresting action, of the Colleges in all great medical inquiries:[61] e.g. Contagion[62] & Lunacy.[63]—In Bethlem hospital it was the rule for some years to give purges & vomits, & to bleed certain classes of the patients at given periods.[64]

Distinction of Typhus & Typhoid Fevers

The dissection by Prost of Parisian Fever-patients in 1804, laid the foundations of our knowledge & turned the attention of pathologists in the direction which has led to such definite results. Petit, Serres, Pommer & Bretonneau followed up the investigations of Prost; but the celebrated treatise of Louis, in 1829, was the first to give a complete & connected view of symptoms as well as of post-mortem lesions in the fever common in Paris.

In 1835 the Academie de Medicine formally proposed the question, what are the

(17)

analogies & the differences between the typhus & typhoid fevers?" The question excited considerable interest in France, but less in England where a strong bias has always prevailed towards a belief in the doctrine of a Single Fever. But dissenters arose. Scotch, English, & American physicians, familiar with the fevers of their own countries, began to visit Paris to study fever there; & they were not long in learning to recognize the chief points of difference between the two fevers. Gerhard & Pennock of Philadelphia, in a systematic treatise were the first to indicate (1836) these differences, it having been already determined that the fever described by Louis under the name of typhoid fever existed in America.⁶⁵ Dr. Watson's⁶⁶ recommendations are

1. *Against* the old plan of "cutting short" the fever at the outset by *emetics* & *cold affusions*.⁶⁷

But emetics perhaps too much neglected, being sometimes

(18)

palliative early where there is gastric disturbance.

Sponging (tepid or cold) instead of affusion. Less eligible in *typhus* than *typhoid*⁶⁸

2. Against blood letting in typhus. He says that according to his experience the fevers which occurred in London before the cholera years 1831–32, not only bore, but required, the abstraction of blood: since then "it has been necessary to abstain wherever we could with safety, from taking blood at all: & still more necessary, even if we take away blood with one hand to uphold the patient with the other: while in the former period, wine & stimulants of all kinds seemed generally superfluous if not pernicious." "Typhoid fever I believe to have been predominant during my earlier, typhus during my later experience."⁶⁹

3. "*Purgatives*—what are we to say in general with respect to them? Intestines should be cleared by an active aperient in the outset.... But if the vital power is much depressed, & when the

(19)

*symptoms threaten ulceration of the intestinal glands, purgatives certainly ought not to be pressed.*⁷⁰

4. Mercury. Experience in favour of it, in the typhoid forms. Against in typhus, i.e. fever characterized by the mulberry rash.⁷¹

5. Cold lotion to head when the heat & aching are great. Bleeding by leeches & cupping.⁷²

6. Mercury in pills, while the character of the fever is uncertain; but when it turns to the typhoid, some opium along with the mercury.

But if the fever be typhus, begin very early with beef tea, ammonia, aether, wine; & omit the mercury.[73]
6. Opiates. Require close watching in small doses.[74]
Incessant vigilance. Boerhaave, in the preface to his Aphorisms professes that he knows of nothing which can be fitly termed a remedy. "Quin solo tempestivo usu tale fiat."[75]

(20)

Bichat's work. "These old writers (Fallopius & Actuarius) were fully possessed (more so than many of their successors) with the two fundamental notions of structural & physiological biology; the 1st, that living beings may be resolved anatomically, into a comparatively small number of structural elements; the 2d, that these elementary parts possess vital properties, which depend for their manifestation only upon the existence of certain general conditions (supply of proper nutriment etc.) & are independent of all direct influence from other parts. . . . It required all the genius of Bichat to sift the wheat from the chaff amongst the great mass of facts which the observation of past ages had accumulated—& strengthening whatever place was weakest by new investigations—to establish these very two propositions . . . —
Huxley, "Cell Theory"[76]

(21)

Substance membraneuse des organes Animaux
"Lorsqu'on a épuisé, par l'eau, par l'alcool, par l'éther, par les acides et alcalis étendus, la chair musculaire, un tissu nerveux, un organe quelconque, il reste une substance blanche comme l'albumine coagulée, mais bien moins élastique, que les alcalis ou les acides concentrés désorganisent ou dépouillent, mais ne dissolvent jamais entièrement" . . .
. . . "C'est là la substance qui, sous le rapport anatomique, joue chez les animaux le même rôle que celle qui forme le tissu cellulaire et vasculaire chez les végétaux, et que je nommerai, dans le courant de cet ouvrage, substance membraneuse, membrane ou substance molle des tissus animaux. C'est elle qui forme la

charpente des grands organes comme des organes microscopiques, des organes mous comme des organes solides, des muscles, des nerfs, des glandes, des os, des cartilages, des tendons et aponévroses, des poils eux-mêmes, enfin

(22)

de tout ce qui, dans un être animé, jouit d'une espèce de végétation, d'un développement vital."[77]

"Les membranes de tous les organes animaux, même les plus disparates par leur fonctions, sont donc d'une homogénéité désespérante pour la physiologie, l'anatomie et la chimie microscopique. Cependant elles peuvent se prêter à des formes capables de fournir des caractères secondaires pour distinguer les différents organes. Nous allons, sous ce rapport, en étudier succinctement etc.[78]

Raspail, 1833

(23)

Mottoes[79]
"Mit kleinen thut man kleine Thaten
Mit grossen wird der Kleine gross"
Goethe

Le sentiment de la fausseté des plaisirs présents, et l'ignorance de la vanité des plaisirs absents causent l'inconstance

Pascal

Whose speech Truth knows not from her thoughts
  Nor love her body from her soul.

G. D. Rossetti

"Thou art a blessed fellow to think as every man thinks; never a man's thought in the world keeps the roadway better than thine."

Shakespeare Henry IV (?)

Passage of the Pestilence. Villemarqué. Barsas Braiz
  "For whoso seeth me first on morrow
  May saine he hath met with sorrow
  For I am sorrow, & sorrow is I."

Chaucer

In all her face no wicked signe
For it was sad, simple & benigne"
                                    Chaucer
                                        over

(24)

Wise in his daily work was he:
   To fruits of diligence
And not to faith or polity
   He plied his utmost sense
The perfect in their little parts
   Whose work is all their prize—
Without them how could Laws or Arts
   Or tower'd cities rise?[80]

Ch. 43. This figure hath high price: 'twas wrought with love
Ages ago in finest ivory:
Nought modish in it, pure & noble lines
Of generous womanhood that fits all time.
That too is costly ware; majolica
of deft design, to please a lordly eye:
The smile, you see, is perfect—,wonderful
As mere faience! A table ornament
To suit the richest mounting.[81]

(25)
Political Dates

Birmingham political Union already founded March 11, 1830, when Mr. Huskisson & Mr. Grant contended for the transfer of representation from East Retford to Birmingham; East Retford having been guilty of bribery.[82]

"Mr O'Connell on the 28th of May moved for leave to bring in a bill to establish Triennial parliaments, universal suffrage & vote by ballot—the foundation of his sytem being this simple but mad proposition, that every man who pays taxes or is liable

to serve in the militia is entitled to have a voice in the representation."
13 members joined him in a house of 332.[83]

Motion to remove the disabilities of Jews, April 1831.[84]
"Mr. Owen had openly declared at a public meeting that Christianity was an imposture."[85]

> Annual Register

(26)

> How oft the sight of means to do the deeds
> Makes ill deeds done!
>> King John[86]

(27)

Capital punishment for sheepstealing abolished 1832 (For forgery not till 1840)[87]

Peruvian bark fell into total discredit in 1799, from its inability to cure the ague; & it was afterwards discovered to have been adulterated with bark of an inferior species.[88]

From Evidence on the State of the Poor Laws (blue book)
Farmer in Sussex pays £160 rent & £120 poor's rates. A good crop of wheat in that county, 4qrs per acre: average crop 2 qrs per acre.
R. Spooner says, in evidence, that the way in which Tithe is collected leads to a great evil. Men are prevented from investing their capital in the cultivation of land because they would thus make their property titheable which it had not been before.
Tithe in a parish in Norfolk—belonging to a corporation at Norwich, who farmed them

(28)

to an Anabaptist, who collected them of a Catholic population & payed £120 to a Protestant Vicar or Curate.[89]

Quarry I

Uses of Manganese; In dyeing & calico printing: in the colouring of glass and enamel; in furnishing oxygen & chlorine. It supplies the cheapest oxygen. Also, it is used in making bleaching powder.[90]

Cholera. "In the end of 1831, the cholera had made its appearance in Sunderland & extended to Newcastle. Instead of moving southwards, it travelled north to Scotland, & appeared suddenly in a very fatal form at Haddington. Approaching Edinburgh it seized upon Musselburgh, six miles from the metropolis, where its ravages were the most severe that had yet been known in the island. In Edinburgh funds had been supplied by voluntary subscription, & labour & attendance by active charity, in clothing & feeding the poor, which, aided by a very vigilant police

(29)

long set the invader at defiance, & when he arrived deprived him of almost all his terror. Hitherto the legislature had been silent. All at once, without apparently having lighted on any intermediate place, the disease appeared in London, & forthwith bills were hurried through parliament (both Houses) vesting in the privy council very ample powers to direct sanatory measures, & authorizing assessments to cover the necessary expenses. In the bill for Scotland the house actually divided on the question whether words which spoke of the disease being an infliction of "providence" should be part of the preamble. Six members, headed by Mr Hume, voted for their exclusion. They had been omitted in the preamble of the English bill, but were inserted in the House of Lords.[91]

Remarks on the History & Treatment of Delirium Tremens. By John Ware, M.D. Boston, 1831

Dr Ware first dogmatically taught that *delirium tremens*

(30)

is a paroxysm of poisoning by alcohol, which in a majority of cases lasts only a given time, & terminates favourably in a critical sleep.[92] He says, "The natural tendency of the paroxysm is to terminate in a spontaneous & salutary sleep at the end of a certain period—viz. sixty to seventy-two hours; & even in the reports of cases which have been submitted to the public as evidences of the efficacy of various modes of practice, sleep has not actually taken place sooner than it would have done in the natural course of the disease.[93] . . . The termination of a paroxysm of delirium tremens is always, as has been already mentioned, in *profound* sleep. . . . Sleep, however, is not always to be regarded as indicating the speedy termination of the paroxysm, since it is not uncommon for patients to sleep a little— from a few minutes to an hour, for instance—on each day of the delirium."[94] Dr Ware

(31)

maintained that in a large proportion of cases with-drawal of the accustomed stimulants had nothing to do with the accessions of the paroxysm, that the disease occurs also in individuals whose habit of drinking has never been suspended at all . . . up to the commencement of the delirium.[95]

(32)

vide. Bacon's advancement of learning
Stowe's London—medical schools?[96]

NOTES TO QUARRY ONE

[1] Names, chiefly of French scientists, taken from Renouard, *History of Medicine*, Eng. trans. (Cincinnati, 1856), or J. R. Russell, *History and Heroes of the Art of Medicine* (London, 1861). Cf. Cross, III: 83, 85. First three lines underlined.

[2] *Lancet*, Sept. 11, 1830, p. 930. This "triumph" was short-lived. On Sept. 11, Wakley (the editor of the *Lancet* and the "medical candidate" referred to) was successful in the "show of hands." Sept. 18 (*Lancet*, p. 963) found the "combat... proceeding in a manner... to afford unbounded satisfaction." But the *Lancet* for Oct. 2 (p. 41) announced that the medical candidate was beaten by a small majority and (pp. 43–49) discussed the contest and its importance.

[3] *Lancet*, Oct. 2, 1830, p. 51.

[4] *Lancet*, June 19, 1830, p. 451, announcement of the project; Oct. 2, pp. 52–54, discussion of its aims.

[5] *Lancet*, Jan. 16, 1830, pp. 538–540; Jan. 23, pp. 371–373, editorial; Apr. 17, p. 85; Apr. 24, p. 132.

[6] The source of this item is unidentified.

[7] *Lancet*, Oct. 9, 1830, p. 69; Oct. 23, p. 129.

[8] *Lancet*, Aug. 28, 1830, p. 878; Oct. 9, p. 71.

[9] *Lancet*, Oct. 2, 1830, p. 60.

[10] *Lancet*, Oct. 30, 1830, p. 168.

[11] *Lancet*, Oct. 9, 1830, p. 84.

[12] William Hone, *The Table Book* (London, 1828), II: 561–562.

[13] *Lancet*, Oct. 16, 1830, pp. 97–103.

[14] *Lancet*, Oct. 16, 1830, p. 113; Oct. 23, p. 145, editorial.

[15] *Lancet*, Sept. 4, 1830, p. 906, review; Oct. 23, pp. 132–135, practical commentary continued in following numbers.

[16] *Lancet*, Oct. 23, 1830, p. 145.

[17] *Lancet*, Oct. 30, 1830, p. 176; Dec. 4, 1830, p. 350; Jan. 15, 1831, p. 533.

[18] *Lancet*, Oct. 30, 1830, p. 180.

[19] *Lancet*, Nov. 6, 1830, pp. 208–209. Letter signed "A Surgeon."

[20] *Lancet*, Nov. 20, 1830, p. 257.

[21] *Lancet*, Nov. 20, 1830, p. 279.

[22] *Lancet*, Sept. 4, 1830, p. 902; Nov. 6, pp. 200–207, full report of the trial; pp. 210–214, 276, editorials; Nov. 13, p. 248, another editorial; Nov. 27, p. 311, Long's trial in second murder case. Cf. p. 7 of *Quarry* and notes.

[23] *Lancet*, Dec. 4, 1830, p. 338. This election of one of the royal dukes in preference to a leading scientist of the day caused the *Lancet's* editor to add, "The Society is rotten to the core." Cf. also, Dec. 25, p. 443.

[24] *Lancet*, Jan. 1, 1831, p. 463. (Inexactly quoted.) The 1831 material really begins here, although the heading "1831" does not occur until p. 8 of the *Quarry*, when a note of April, 1831, is given.

[25] *Lancet*, Jan. 1, 1831, pp. 463–464.

[26] *Lancet*, Jan. 1, 1831, pp. 470–471.

[27] *Lancet*, Oct. 23, 1830, book received; Jan. 8, 1831, pp. 485–487, discussion.

[28] *Lancet*, Jan. 8, 1831, p. 503. Cf. D'Arcy Power, "Medicine in the British Isles," in *Clio Medica* (New York: Hoeber, 1930), p. 12. "The scots universities always more active in medical education than Oxford and Cambridge—great teachers, many students."

²⁹ *Lancet*, Jan. 15, 1831, pp. 531–532, scale of fees suggested by the Newcastle and Gateshead Association; March 12, 1831, p. 782, comment on letter by T. M. Greenhow about the suggested scale. In the *Lancet* of Jan. 8, 1831, pp. 506–507, appears a list of fees in use in New York, taken from "Sketch of the State of Medicine in America" by Dr. Black of Bolton.

³⁰ *Lancet*, Jan. 22, 1831, p. 567. A very condensed and rather garbled summary of a lengthy discussion.

³¹ *Lancet*, Jan. 29, 1831, pp. 596–598. Very much condensed note on a long editorial showing the injustice of demands by the College of Surgeons.

³² *Lancet*, Feb. 26, 1831, pp. 725–726. Long was being tried again, this time for the "murder" of Mrs. Colin Campbell Lloyd. He was acquitted.

³³ *Lancet*, Feb. 26, 1831, p. 726.

³⁴ *Lancet*, Apr. 30, 1831, pp. 151–154. This note is the first one labeled "1831," but see note 24.

³⁵ *Lancet*, Mar. 26, 1831, p. 865. The meeting was held March 16, Wakley speaking at length and giving a sketch of the history of the three "medical corporations" afterward printed in the *Lancet*.

³⁶ *Lancet*, Mar. 26, 1831, pp. 851–852. Some of the remarks about hospitals are quoted from W. Lawrence, M.D., *Speeches Delivered at Two Meetings of Members of the Royal College of Surgeons* (London, 1826).

³⁷ The *Lancet* for part of 1831, most of 1832, and part of 1833 was crowded with discussions of the cholera. I find no one page or section from which this note was drawn. The *Annual Register* may have furnished some of the items. Cf. *Quarry I*, pp. 28–29.

³⁸ The scientists named so far on this page all appear in Huxley's essay quoted from on page 20 of the *Quarry*. In George Eliot's journal for September 10, 1869, she writes, "... reading on medical subjects—Encyclopedia about the Medical Colleges, 'Cullen's Life,' Russell's 'Heroes of Medicine,' etc." We cannot be sure that it was the *Encyclopaedia Britannica* which she referred to, but it is probable. If she found the Encyclopedia useful on the "medical colleges," she might have found it handy in straightening out the list of scientists who had made history in the use of the microscope. Lewes could, no doubt, have furnished her with a sketch of the subject; we have to remember that she had ever at hand that source of ready information.

³⁹ Huxley also mentions Cuvier's respect for Wolff, but does not give Cuvier's tribute to Swammerdamm quoted here. I have not found its source. Either Lewes or the Encyclopedia—or both—may have given her the facts about the 18th-century anatomists, Lyonnet and Hewson. Lyonnet appears in the *Encyclopaedia Britannica*, 8th ed., IX: 5; Hewson in II: 766. As the 8th edition of the *Britannica* came out in 1860, it would seem an up-to-date and reliable source of information.

⁴⁰ Gleichen is mentioned in the *Britannica*, 8th ed., III, 208, in connection with Ehrenberg's work.

⁴¹ This paper of Robert Brown's also mentions Gleichen's work, cf. *Miscellaneous Botanical Works of Robert Brown*, published by the Ray Society, 1866, p. 477. The article in question, "A Brief Account of Microscopical Observations Made in the Months of June, July and August, 1827, . . . etc.," *Miscellaneous Works*, I: 463–486, is marked on the title page "published," but dated at the end, p. 479, "July 30, 1828." In the following article, "Additional Remarks on Active Molecules," dated July 28, 1829, Brown says, p. 479, "About twelve months ago I printed an account of Microscopical Observations made in the summer of 1827." This privately printed article or,

possibly, the "Additional Remarks" must have been what "inspired" Ehrenberg before he set out on his journey of 1829. The facts cited by George Eliot on pages 9 and 10 of the *Quarry* may have been given her by Lewes, but the passage beginning "Period between Leeuwenhoek and Ehrenberg . . ." *sounds* as if it were quoted from a book or from an article. Some day I trust this source will be found.

⁴² The only copy of this work available in the United States is in the library of the College of Physicians in Philadelphia. The full title adds at the end, "in London." It was published in London in the year given.

⁴³ *Exposition*, pp. 18-19.
⁴⁴ *Ibid.*, pp. 20-21.
⁴⁵ *Ibid.*, p. 22. The last phrase, "by which the Bishop's License" etc., was added by George Eliot in explanation, referring to p. 18.
⁴⁶ *Ibid.*, pp. 18-19.
⁴⁷ *Ibid.*, pp. 24-25.
⁴⁸ *Ibid.*, p. 27.
⁴⁹ *Ibid.*, p. 28.
⁵⁰ *Ibid.*, p. 67.
⁵¹ *Ibid.*, p. 131. After "College" in line 1, George Eliot omitted "having performed prodigies against the empirics in town"; after "practise" in line 3, she omitted "physic." For the locating of this quotation and the two following I am indebted to Mr. W. B. McDaniel, II, Librarian of the College of Physicians in Philadelphia.
⁵² *Ibid.*, p. 175. In the *Exposition* the passage reads, ". . . by a private college, which cannot even confer the title of doctor." The parenthesis adds George Eliot's own comment.
⁵³ *Ibid.*, pp. 175-176. The original reads, ". . . graduates of Oxford and Cambridge, since they were deemed by the college themselves to be entitled to the exclusive privilege of the fellowship."
⁵⁴ *Ibid.*, p. 196.
⁵⁵ *Ibid.*, p. 194.
⁵⁶ *Ibid.*, p. 221.
⁵⁷ *Ibid.*, p. 222.
⁵⁸ *Ibid.*, pp. 222-223.
⁵⁹ *Ibid.*, p. 223.
⁶⁰ *Ibid.*, pp. 238-240. The last remark is George Eliot's own comment.
⁶¹ *Ibid.*, p. 249 ff.
⁶² *Ibid.*, p. 261.
⁶³ *Ibid.*, p. 263.
⁶⁴ *Ibid.*, pp. 264-265.
⁶⁵ W. W. Gerhard, "On the Typhus Fever Which Occurred at Philadelphia in the Spring and Summer of 1836," *American Journal of the Medical Sciences*, XIX (February, 1837): 219-322; XX (August, 1837): 289-322. Of Pennock's connection with the study Gerhard writes (p. 295 of the first article): "Our inquiries were conducted so much in concert . . . that this memoir is in most respects the expression of the results obtained by our joint labours." In the *American Journal of the Medical Sciences*, XV (February, 1835): 320, Dr. Gerhard had published "Reports of Cases Treated in the Medical Wards of the Pennsylvania Hospital. Part 1st. Typhus and Remittent Fevers." In this study he had identified the Philadelphia fever with the Paris fever described by Louis.

⁶⁶ (Sir) Thomas Watson, *Lectures on the Principles and Practice of Physic* ... (Philadelphia, 1844).

⁶⁷ *Ibid.*, p. 856.

⁶⁸ *Ibid.*, p. 857.

⁶⁹ *Ibid.*, p. 857.

⁷⁰ *Ibid.*, pp. 857–858.

⁷¹ *Ibid.*, p. 858.

⁷² *Ibid.*, p. 858.

⁷³ *Ibid.*, pp. 858–859.

⁷⁴ *Ibid.*, pp. 859–860. A very brief summary of a long passage. Note the repetition of the number "6."

⁷⁵ *Ibid.*, p. 861. The *Quarry* note seems to read "Quia," but the "a" may be an "n." "Quin" is what Watson used, following Boerhaave correctly.

⁷⁶ *British and Foreign Medical and Chirurgical Review*, XII (1853): 285–314. In Leonard Huxley's biography of T. H. Huxley (I: 152) the date of this article is given as 1858, doubtless a printer's error. Leonard Huxley quotes Sir Michael Foster's remark on the inspiration which many medical students drew from this essay. It was signed T. H. Huxley. The names of some of the scientists mentioned in this review, i.e., Leuwenhock (so spelled by Huxley), Malpighi, Schleiden, and Schwann, are included in the list (*Quarry*, p. 9) of those who forwarded "microscopical discovery." The note on Bichat's work appears on page 289 of the review.

⁷⁷ F. V. Raspail, *Nouveau système de chimie organique fondé sur des nouvelles méthodes d'observation*, etc. Troisième édition, etc. (Bruxelles, 1839), I: 362. The first edition of this work, published in 1833, is not available in this country at present. There are a few minor differences in wording between the 1833 text and that of 1839, as far as we can judge by the *Quarry* notes, but the substance of the passages remains the same.

⁷⁸ *Ibid.*, p. 364.

⁷⁹ Most of the quotations noted down on this page were not used in *Middlemarch*. They were taken from George Eliot's familiar reading. The two lines from Goethe are written above two lines which are scratched out and undecipherable. The quotation from Pascal was used for the heading of chapter 75.

⁸⁰ Used at the beginning of chapter 40 in *Middlemarch*. In the *Quarry*, line 3 originally read, "not to sounding polity." The *Quarry* quote says that the verse is "From a Black Letter Inscription." But this statement is crossed out and we are left to speculate as to its source. It is hard to believe that it came from any pen but George Eliot's; certainly it has no flavor of a "Black Letter Inscription." The quotation as given in the novel has been properly punctuated; "faith" has been changed to "faiths," "*the* perfect," line 5, has been changed to "*these* perfect."

⁸¹ These lines were printed at the beginning of chapter 45 practically without change. Anyone familiar with George Eliot's ideas and verse style would, I think, be fairly confident that she wrote this very pat description herself, though the Browning tone is quite obvious.

⁸² *Annual Register*, LXXII (1830): 91.

⁸³ *Annual Register*, LXXII (1830): 105.

⁸⁴ One of the recurring efforts to give political equality to the Jews; for example, the *Annual Register*, LXXII (1830): 109, records one. In LXXV (1833): 226 we find another: "the Jews alone were now the only class ... whose religion affected their rights. Mr. Grant brought in a bill to relieve them of all civil disabilities." This bill passed the Commons, but was thrown out at the second reading by the Lords.

Notes to Quarry I

[85] *Annual Register*, LXXII (1830): 113.

[86] These lines might have served at the head of chapter 70, but were rejected in favor of some which voice one of George Eliot's deepest beliefs, in the force of inner character as opposed to outer circumstance.

[87] The source of this is unidentified. It could have come from any account of reform in the criminal laws.

[88] I have not found the source of this quotation.

[89] I cannot give any exact source for this quotation. Material related to it is to be found in *Reports of Commissioners*, Vol. I, *First Annual Report of the Poor Law Commissioners*, 2d ed. (London, 1836), pp. 51–55. The *Annual Register*, LXXVI (1834): 209–213, discusses the church rates. The same volume, pp. 214–219, discusses tithes, stressing (p. 217) the "tendency [of the tithe system] to check the investment of capital in the improvement of land."

[90] Any dictionary or cyclopedia could have supplied this information.

[91] *Annual Register*, LXXIV (1832): 274. The amount of space devoted to cholera in the pages of the *Lancet* may be taken as an indication of the anxiety with which the medical profession regarded the epidemic of 1832 in England. Volume II for 1830–1831 has a half column in the index devoted to "Cholera"; Vol. I, 1831–1832, has three and a half columns; Vol. II, 1831–1832, has *four columns;* Vol. I, 1832–1833, has one and a half columns; Vol. II, 1832–1833, has less than half a column. For an account of this epidemic see E. Ashworth Underwood, "The History of the 1832 Cholera Epidemic in Yorkshire," *Proceedings of the Royal Society of Medicine*, section *History of Medicine*, 1934–1935. This article is listed in the *Isis* bibliography for December, 1936, p. 263, with a note by Dr. H. R. Viets: Epidemic in the east, 1817, appeared England 1831. 1832 saw 1960 deaths in Yorkshire, one-half of them in Leeds. In 1832 the disease was entirely unknown to British practitioners. Sanitary reform began shortly after this epidemic. Full list of references to contemporary medical reports.

[92] John Ware, M.D., "Remarks on the History and Treatment of Delirium Tremens," from *Transactions of the Massachusetts Medical Society* (Boston, 1831), p. 11.

[93] *Ibid.*, p. 45. Roughly quoted; sentence structure changed to permit condensation.

[94] *Ibid.*, p. 33.

[95] *Ibid.*, p. 7. On page 49 Dr. Ware writes: "There is in this disease, as in some others, a happy insensibility of the system to the action of remedies, which allows it, in a large majority of instances, to take its own course essentially unaffected by them. It may seem presumptuous to make this statement in the face of such authorities as have written on this disease. But many, if not all, have taken it for granted that it is to be treated by medicine; they have never trusted to the spontaneous efforts of nature for a cure." George Eliot must have noticed this statement. Its bearing on Lydgate's conduct of Raffles's case is obvious.

[96] This note, which is on the first flyleaf at the back of the notebook, obviously belongs with *Quarry I*.

Quarry Two

[Second flyleaf, recto]

Dissolution of Parlt. April 22, 1831
General rejoicing & illuminations. Elections, May.
Parlt. Reopened, June 21.[1]

[Second flyleaf, verso]

Dates

1830 opening of Liverpool & Manchr. Railway, April
" George IV died, June 26—Whigs come in
" French Revolution,* July, 27, 28, 29,
" Parliament Dissolved,† July 24
" King & Queen decline to visit the city, Nov. 9. Funds fall.
" Mr. Brougham's motion for Reform   Nov. 16.
" Tory amendment carried. Machine breaking
"   x   (Writs returnable for
1831 Parliament dissolved April 22 & gen. election. Reopened.
   June 21
"   x   First cases of Cholera
" (Paganini) Reform Bill thrown out by the Lords Oct. 7
" Bristol Riots Oct. 29
   Reintrod. 3d time Dec. 12
1832 Cholera appears at Rotherhithe & London Feb. & Sep.
   R.B. read in the Lords, Mar. Motion against it carried May 7‡
" Reform Bill passed, June 7.
" Capl. Punishment for sheep & cattle stealing abolished.
" First Nos. of Chambers' Journal & Penny Mag.
1833 Reformed Parliament, election Jan.
" Thanksgiving for departure of Cholera, Ap. 14[2]

---

* Charles X published the Ordinances July 26, withdrew them, 29. "Too late!" said Laffitte, "Since yesterday, a century has passed away.
† Deaths from Cholera in Paris, Feb. & Mar., 1832—18,402
‡ King threatening to create new peers, May 18   Carried in the Lords June 4
[1] For numbered notes to *Quarry II* see pages 65–66 below.

(1)
Queries

Periods of university examinations

	Oxford	Cambridge
Lent term	Jan. 14–April 1	Jan 13–Mar. 31
Easter	Ap. 12–May 26	April 14–June 23
Trinity	May 27–July 8	
Mich.	Oct. 10–Dec. 18	Oct. 1–Dec. 16

Notes from a letter on Hospitals

Chaplain. Chaplain at C honorary. Came when sent for & occasionally otherwise. At S. salaried £40.& had regular services &nd visitations.

Matron. At C factotum. At S. Housekeeper, with only power to report Nurses to the House Surgeon, who engaged or dismissed them.

House Surgeon. Always considered to carry out the treatment of the Surgeons & Physns, to attend urgent cases etc on his own account, & to keep the medical part of the house in order. Not allowed to attend cases out of the Hospital.

Physns. & Surgns. Attendance usually in forenoon ("At no decent institution is the term medical officer used as in C. viz. to express a license to attend medical & surgical cases—in fact to attend the Hospl as general practitioners

(2)[3]

Dr B. in 1869 refused to give a testimonial for the C. Hospital on the ground that such a state of things ought not to exist."[4]

Middlemarch

Directors

Mr. Plymdale, Dyer	Votes for Tyke
Mr. Powderell, Retired ironmonger	" "
Mr. Hawley, Lawyer & town clerk	" Farebrother

Quarry II 45

Mr. Hackbutt, Tanner " Farebrother
Mr. Larcher, Carrier   Tyke
Rev. E. Thesiger, Rector of St. Peter's   Tyke
Arthur Brooke Esq. of Tipton Grange   Tyke
Nicholas Bulstrode, Esq. Banker   Tyke[5]

    Lowick
o
      2 miles
        Middlemarch
o
        3 miles
           Tipton
          o
      o
    Freshitt

[Pen-drawn lines connect the places indicated by small circles]

(3)
Relations to be developed

1 of Dorothea to Mr. Casaubon
2 " Lydgate to Rosamond
3 " Fred Vincy to Mary Garth
4 " The Vincys to Old Featherstone
5 " Dorothea to Will Ladislaw
6 " Lydgate to Bulstrode
7 " Bulstrode to John Raffles
8 " Celia to Sir James
9 " Ladislaw to Mr Brooke
10 " Caleb Garth to Mr Brooke etc.
11 " Mr Farebrother to all, except Sir J. & Mr Brooke

(4)
Private dates[6]

Dorothea married, 1827. Featherstone dies & Ladislaw comes to Tipton, Ap. 1830. Celia married May Lydgate's marriage 1830—July or August

Mr Brooke tries for Parliament May 1831
Mr Casaubon's death, 1831. March
Celia's baby born, 1831—April
Dorothea's second marriage, 1832 Jan. or Feb.
Child born, 1833
Rosamond's baby born, June 1, 1831
Bulstrode buys Stone Court, June or July 1831
Raffles comes back, July 1831
Raffles dies, Aug. 1832. Two years after Lydgate's marriage.
    "   "   "

 Mr Casaubon's Death, March 1831
 Dorothea settled at Lowick again June 1831
Bulstrode & Raffles at Stone Court, end of June 1831
 Fred Vincy's adventure & choice July 1831
 Lydgate's disclosure of trouble to Rosd. Aug.

(5)[7]

Middlemarch. Part I. Miss Brooke. Decr.

Chapter 1 The two sisters pp 1–13
   2 Mr Casaubon & Sir James come to dine. 13–23
   3 The two suitors persevere 23–36
   4 Dorothea's eyes opened. A letter arrives 36–45
   5 Mr Casaubon accepted 45–57
   6 Mrs Cadwallader informed, & Sir James 57–70
   7. Dorothea reads with Mr Casaubon 70–75
   8. Sir James appeals to the Rector 75–82
   9. Dorothea sees Lowick, & Will Ladislaw 82–92
   10. The marriage approaching, & a party 92–103
   11 Lydgate talked of at Fred Vincy's breakfast
   12 Rosamond & Fred ride to Stone Court & Mr Featherstone asks for something awkward.
Ms. 134 pp.

(6)

Middlemarch Part II. Old and young. Feb.

Ch XI Lydgate is a subject of conversation at [*written above:* in] the Vincys' dining room, as the new doctor, 103–112

Quarry II

    XII Fred & Rosamond go to Stone Court. Old F. asks for something awkward. Rosd. sees Lydgate—135⁸
   XIII. Bulstrode with Lydgate & Vincy. 135–145
   XIV Fred carries a note to his uncle. Tells Mary of his love. Gives £80 to his mother to keep 145–160
    XV Lydgate's history and present ambition 160–173
   XVI Lydgate dines at Mr Vincy's. 173–189
  XVII. Mr Farebrother at home. XVIII Tyke elected 189–220
   XIX Fred Vincy tries to meet his debt 220–237⁹
    XX Fred has to confess to Mr & Mrs Garth 237–246
   XXI Fred confesses to Mary, & her father comes 246–256

Ch.   XIX Mrs Casaubon in the Vatican Museum
    XX Dorothea in tears. Receives a visitor
   XXI Mr & Mrs Casaubon go to see a studio

MS. 126 pp.

(7)¹⁰

Part III. April

Ch.   22 Fred Vincy tries to meet his debt
       23 Has to confess to Mr & Mrs Garth
       24 Fred confesses to Mary & her father comes
       25 Fred taken ill, & Mr Wrench dismissed
       26 Lydgate & Rosamond in flirtation
       27 Mr & Mrs Casaubon return to Lowick
       28 Mr Casaubon taken ill
       29 Lydgate advises & Mr Brooke writes a letter
       30 The flirtation of Lydgate ends in engagement
       31 The blood-relations at Stone Court
       32 Old Featherstone's death

(8)¹¹

Part III. April

Waiting for Death

Ch   22 Scene in the Museum of the Vatican
Tr   23 Dorothea in tears. Is called on by a relative

48   Quarry for Middlemarch

to   24 Mr & Mrs Casaubon go to see a studio
pII   [25 *cancelled*]
        27 They return to Lowick
       [26 *cancelled*]
        28 Mr. Casaubon taken ill
       [27 *cancelled*]
        29 Lydgate advises, & Mr Brooke writes a letter
       [28 *cancelled*]
        25 Fred is taken ill, & Mr Wrench dismissed
   29 26 Lydgate & Rosamond in flirtation
        30. The flirtation ends in engagement
        31. The blood-relations at Stone Court
        32 Old Featherstone unable to do as he likes at the last

      ch22 Fred Vincy tries to meet his debt
         23 Has to confess to Mr & Mrs Garth
         24 Fred confesses to Mary; & her father comes.
              MS. 150 pages

(9)

Motives[12]

Featherstone's burial. Arrival of Ladislaw
Will read, & Family consternation
Advent of the new stranger, Rigg
Lydgate & Rosamond married
Mr Brooke seen to be making political tentatives. Ladislaw's relation to Dorothea & Mr Casaubon shown, a propos of appointment to edit the Pioneer.
Dismay of Sir James & the Cadwalladers.
Attacks on Mr Brooke as a Landlord.
He is induced to give the management of his estate to Caleb Garth
What Fred Vincy does.
   How Lydgate goes on medically, & in relation to Bulstrode & the Hospital vide P. V
Looming of Raffles

Quarry II

(10)

Part IV. June. Three Love Problems.

Ch. 33 Featherstone buried & Ladislaw resuscitated
" 34. The Reading of the Will.
" 35. Lydgate & Rosamond advance toward marriage
" 36 Ladislaw's settlement at Middlemarch, in relation
" " to Dorothea & Mr Casaubon.
" 37 Sir James & the Cadwalladers attack Mr Brooke about
" " the management of the farms 249a
" 38 Dorothea goes to the Grange, & Dagley has his say 266
" 39 Caleb Garth at breakfast etc. 287
" 40 Mr Raffles visits Mr Rigg 296
" 41 Mr Casaubon in prospect of death.

pp. 164[13]

(11)[14]

Motives (in general)

Mr Casaubon dies.
Mr Brooke stands & falls
Embarrassment of Lydgate
Raffles comes on the scene
Scandal in Middlemarch
Raffles' Death
Lydgate accepts money from Bulstrode
Further scandal
Blight on Bulstrode & Lydgate
   Rosamond's flirtation with Ladislaw
? Dorothea after severe struggles goes to Rosamond
? Action of Caleb Garth & Mr Farebrother

Continuation of Part V

1. About Mr Farebrother's appointment to Lowick
2. Mr Brooke goes to the hustings
3. Fred Vincy's choice of a career
4. Raffles' return ?
5. Drama of Will & Dorothea advanced

(12)[15]

Part V August. The Dead Hand

Chap.	41		Lydgate consulted by Mr Casaubon. Scene between Dorothea & her husband.
	43	42	Dorothea goes into Middlemarch: calls at Lydgate's
	44	43	Dorothea & Lydgate talk of the Hospital
	45	44	Lydgate's medical position: scene between him & Rosamond.
	46	45	Mr Brooke & Ladislaw. Lydgate & Ladislaw.
	47	"	Will goes to Lowick Church
	48		Mr Casaubon's last wishes
		49	Mr Casaubon dies
49	49	50	Sir James & Mr Brooke confer about the Will
50	50	51	Celia "prepares" Dorothea, & Lydgate exerts his influence for Mr Farebrother.
51	52	"	Mr Brooke addresses the electors.
52	53		Mr Farebrother performs a difficult duty.
	53.		Raffles reappears

MS. pages 151

(13)

Part VI October: The Widow & the Wife

Ch.	54.	Interview & goodbye between Dorothea & Will.
	55.	Dorothea declares she shall not remarry.
	56.	Fred Vincy chooses his vocation.
	57	Lydgate embarrassed. Scene with R.
	58.	Fred Vincy becomes jealous.
	59.	Rosamond tells Will about the codicil
60	60	The Sale. Raffles recognizes Will
61	61	Interview between Will & Bulstrode.
	62	Interview between Will & Dorothea.

MS. pp. 156.

Quarry II

(14)

Part VII. December
Two Temptations.

- Chap. 63. New Year. Mr Farebrother & Lydgate   12
- 64. Lydgate & Rosamond: house-letting   37
- 65 Sir Godwin's letter comes.   45
- 66 Lydgate in the Billiard Room: Fred called by Mr Farebrother   60
- 67 Lydgate applies to Bulstrode   72
- 68 Bulstrode's late experience, & consequent plans.   85
- 69 Caleb Garth informs Bulstrode that Raffles is at Stone Court. Lydgate called in. Goes home & finds the execution in his house.
- 70 Bulstrode's state of mind about Raffles—& Lydgate. Gives Lydgate the cheque for 1000. Struggles. Gives the key to the housekeeper. *Death.*
- 71 Scandal in Middlemarch. Mr. Hawley's outburst against Bulstrode. Dorothea enters.

MS. pp. 149

(15)

Part VIII. February
Sunset & Sunrise.

- Ch.72   Dorothea wants to help Lydgate—.
- 73   Lydgate's first anguish
- 74   Mrs Bulstrode learns her sorrow
- 75   Rosamond & Lydgate
- 76   Lydgate & Dorothea.
- 77   Dorothea, Rosamond & Will Ladislaw
- 78   Will & Rosamond [*interlineated, underscored:* 79] afterwards Will & Lydgate
- [79 *cancelled*]
- 80 Dorothea in her anguish.   90
- 81 Dorothea & Rosamond.   105
- 82 Will Ladislaw   112

83 Will & Dorothea   123
84 Mr Brooke carries news   138
85 Mr & Mrs Bulstrode   143
86

(16)
Garth Family

Mary 22; Christy, at Glasgow, 19, Alfred, 15
James 12; Ben, 10, Letty 8.

Bulstrode 58
Raffles 51
Joshua Rigg 32
His mother 56

(17)
Sketch I.

Bulstrode, when young, was a banker's clerk in London & member of a dissenting church to wh. a wealthy couple living at Highbury also belonged. The husband had a business in the city, & on Bulstrode becoming an intimate offered him a place as clerk & accountant; which would be more profitable than his actual situation. Bulstrode accepted & found that the business was a pawnbroker's connected with the receipt of stolen goods.

Preliminary conversations had warned him that the wife was unacquainted with the nature of the business, & the facts were gradually opened to him as necessities which had crept into the management & could not be done away with.

Bulstrode showed ability, & became a confidential associate, winning his way at the same time with the pious wife on the ground of his gifts & divine grace.

(18)
Sketch II.

The couple had had three children, but the two sons had died, & this bereavement made them relent towards the daughter who had run away from them to go on the stage, & had married.

But this daughter had disappeared, & they knew no means of recovering her except by advertisement, which had hitherto failed, but was persevered in.

Quarry II 53

Meanwhile, the husband died, & after a short time Bulstrode won the favour of the widow, who, however, before she made the settlements preliminary to her second marriage, was increasingly anxious to find her daughter & her daughter's possible offspring. Bulstrode, on the other hand, thought this extremely undesirable, as a possible diversion of her property into a less useful channel.

If she married him, he intended

(19)

Sketch III.

as occasion served, to draw away the capital from the criminal business & use it more irreproachably. But the advertising could not be evaded, or an apparent sympathy with the widow's wish.

Still there was no result. But at this stage of affairs a man named Raffles who had early been in service at Highbury but was now a subordinate in the city business was sent on some occasion to Dieppe, & there saw a young couple with their child, the man apparently in a reduced state from sickness, the woman closely resembling the girl whom Raffles had known as the pawnbroker's daughter & whom he knew to have been advertised for. She was holding her baby in her arms & showed a wedding ring.

Raffles came forward & said, "I beg pardon, ma'am, but was your name

(20)

Sketch IV.

Sarah Yorke? & did your parents live at Highbury?" She coloured, was startled & said "Yes." But Raffles then drew back, saying, "I thought so," & left them. He knew that the marriage was pending between Bulstrode & the widow York, & hence debated with himself to which of the two he should carry his information. He determined for Bulstrode, conjecturing that he should get more money there for silence than in the other direction for speech, & in no case should he lose the claim for speech ultimately.

Bulstrode told Raffles that he himself would mention the matter: it was necessary to inquire into things & be cautious, for the sake of the widow's feelings. On certain hints from Raffles, he observed that R. had done a good

(21)
Sketch V.

service which should be well rewarded if he remained silent. After this, the advertising ceased, & Bulstrode married the widow, but not before Raffles had so presented the question to Bulstrode that he had secured a large sum in acquittance & had gone off to America.

Not long after the marriage the widow died, Bulstrode wound up the business & sought a position in the provinces; having among other changes, left the dissenting body & found all the edification he needed in the evangelical party of the Establishment.

The child of that couple is Will Ladislaw whose father is the son of Mr Casaubon's aunt Julia & her Polish husband, & inherits from the latter artistic faculties. In his extremity of illness & poverty he makes himself known to Mr Casaubon, having family guarantees, & from that time

(22)
Sketch VI.

Mr Casaubon provides for the mother & Will, the father having shortly died. Will's mother, Sarah York, had run away from home to go on the stage under peculiar circumstances, not only following a bent in opposition to her mother's dissenting tastes, but proximately determined by learning from a spiteful rejected suitor that her father's trade was dishonorable. Hence the choice of her husband's friends as sources of help, rather than her own, was doubly determined.

[The idea which governs the plot about Bulstrode is, that there is nothing which the law can lay hold of to make him responsible for: the Nemesis is wrought out by the public opinion determined against him.]

Quarry II

(23)

How Ladislaw goes on in Middlemarch
Initiates relation to Rosamond
Scene of Fred Vincy's choice, after Mar. 31
Ladislaw's birth known
Mr Farebrother's appointment to the living

(24)
Elements.

1. Mr Casaubon makes the arrangements about his will, having been stimulated by Lydgate's answers to his inquiries about his health.
2. Lydgate again in colloquy with Dorothea, whence an occasion for her to apply some money.
3. Collision between Lydgate & medical men connected with Bulstrode.
4. Leading up to Mr Brooke's nomination in *April or May*
β 1831; his failure & loss of appetite for a public career.
5. Mr Casaubon's death. Sir James & Celia
6. Fred Vincy's debate about his career
7 δ Arrival of Raffles
8 Embarrassments of Lydgate
9 Second marriage of Dorothea
10 ε Lydgate attends Raffles' deathbed
11 Accepts money from Bulstrode
12 Scandal blighting him & Bulstrode

(25)[16]
Political dates

After the accession of William IV. Parliament was dissolved on the 23d. July. The writs were made returnable on the 14th. of September. Parliament opened Nov. 2. Duke of Wellington's declaration against reform.

King & Queen refuse to dine in the city, Nov. 9. Government defeated on Sir H. Parnell's motion for inquiry into the Civil List, Nov. 14

Brougham, having pledged himself to his constituency to bring forward a bill for reform had on the opening of Parliament given notice of a motion to that effect. Hence, lest they should be defeated on this question also, the ministry resigned. Lord Grey as prime minister explained his policy, Nov. 22.
Parliament reassembled after Xmas, Feb. 3 1831
Lord John Russell brought forth his measure of Reform on the 1st. of March. On Ap. 21, Ministers defeated on Mr. Bankes's motion to adjourn, Ap. 22. Parliament dissolved.

(26)

Elements of B. VI.

First meeting between Will & Dorothea after her husband's death
Will's increasing intimacy with the Lydgates
Lydgate gets more embarrassed, & moody in consequence
Rosamond makes him angry by writing to his uncle.
Will & Dorothea meet again & part with a sense that they can't marry, Will knowing all.
Rosamond flirting with Will.
Fred Vincy choosing his career

(27)

Will Ladislaw & Dorothea

An offence springs up between Mr Brooke & Will
Will, going on as editor of the Pioneer, comes to Lowick to see the Farebrothers, & has an interview with Dorothea. They part with a sense of being divided by destiny.

Dorothea has projects about filling her life: tells Sir James & Celia that she will never be married again—Celia's boy will have everything. She will go on some heroic errand of carrying away emigrants etc. Meanwhile, the cholera. Will does not go away & gets more intimate with Mrs. Lydgate. Learns the nature of Mr Casaubon's codicil; also about his mother's family from Bulstrode. There is another meeting & parting between him & Dorothea. She finds him with Mrs Lydgate. Scene between her & Will—anger, jealousy, reproach, ending in Dorothea's passionate avowal, & declaration that she will never marry him. Will reproaches Rosamond with having ruined his happiness. Rosamond alarmed lest Dorothea should tell Lydgate. Dorothea goes to R. having conquered her jealousy by pity, & hears that Will has been true to her.[17]

(28)

Bulstrode & Raffles

Bulstrode buys Featherstone's land; Rigg having an ideal elsewhere. Raffles, not knowing where to find Bulstrode, his letter being dated from "The Shrubs" & containing no clue, comes again after Rigg, & finds Bulstrode riding about Stone Court. Rigg's ideal is a money-changing business.

Raffles comes again, recognizes Will & tells Bulstrode, who gets Raffles away by payment, & then under conscientious relenting offers amends to Will.

Raffles comes back the third time.

(29)[18]

Scenes

1. First interview between Will & Dorothea after her husband's death.
2. Dorothea tells Sir James & Celia that she will not marry again. Entertaining projects of usefulness.
3. Fred Vincy has an adventure.
4. In consequence seeks employment with Mr Garth.
5. Lydgate embarrassed more & more, is moody. Rosamond, discontented, writes to Sir Godwin. Sir Godwin replies to Lydgate. His anger with R.
6. Will, not going away, gets more intimate with Rosamond, & she more disposed to conquer him.
7. Will learns the nature of Mr Casaubon's Will
8. Raffles comes back & recognizes Will
9. Raffles tells Bulstrode who Will is.
10. Bulstrode paying Raffles to go away, makes offers to Will, constrained by fear & conscience.*

---

* Bulstrode expecting to be cramped for money induces Dorothea to do more for the Hospital

11 Will's struggles. Gets an interview with Dorothea. They part.
12 Will vacillating goes to Rosamond
13 Dorothea discovers them in emotion—together

(30)
Scenes

14 Scene of anger & jealousy between Will & Dorothea, ending in her avowal of love & resolve not to marry him
15 Will goes to Rosamond & reproaches her with having ruined his happiness.
16 Dorothea, wrought on by compassion, goes to Rosamond, & so moves her that R. tells D. how Will has been true.
17 Meeting & final reconciliation of Will & Dorothea.
18 Dorothea declares to Sir James her intention to marry Will
19. Lydgate in difficulties has half made up his mind to ask Dorothea for aid, & learns that she is going to marry Will.
20 Raffles comes back. Terror of Bulstrode. Disclosures.
21 Raffles' death. Bulstrode gives Lydgate £1000.
22 Scandal in Middlemarch. Blight on Lydgate & Bulstrode....

Epilogue

23 Dorothea in her second married life (in London ?)

(31)
How to End the Parts

Part VI ends with the Farebrothers telling Dorothea of Will's sudden departure—
  VII. Ends with Lydgate's bribe [*written in above:* outpouring] to Dorothea
VIII. Epilogue of reconciliation with Dorothea's family
                "   "   "

Remaining Scenes of Part VI.

1. Fred goes to see the Garth Family, finds Mary still away at Lowick.
2. Fred walks to Lowick & sees Mary
3. After Will has learned the nature of Mr Casaubon's codicil.

Quarry II

4 Raffles returns & recognizes Will & tells Bulstrode.
5. Scene between Bulstrode & Will
6. Will's struggles
7 Interview between Will & Dorothea. Parting
8. Will gone away.

(32)

Sketch 2.

Will declares his indifference as to what becomes of him & what career he shall pursue since the only woman he loves is debarred from him by honour. Departs.

Mrs. Cadwallader lets drop some phrase indicating some flirtation between Mrs Lydgate & Will, (in Dorothea's hearing).

Scene between Lydgate & Dorothea in which he exposes his whole life. Estrangement between him & Rosamond—her indifference to everything but Ladislaw & his singing etc.

Dorothea writes to him lending the sum: takes it herself to his house that it may fall into no other hands: also wishing to speak to Rosamond in the way of counsel—

Meanwhile Will has returned impatient to hear something about Dorothea

Calls on Lydgate. Rosamond who has been pining for him, overjoyed at his presence—thinks it is for her & pours out her feeling

Means to go to Utopia.

(33)

Mr Farebrother comes to Lydgate to see if anything can be done for him. Finds him in high spirits, released from trouble. Hears him speak of Raffles' illness.

α Bambridge tells what he has heard
β Raffles identified as just buried
γ Diffusion of the scandal among the Middlemarchers in connexion with Lydgate's release from debt
δ Scandal spreads to Freshitt & Lowick
ε Mr Hawley explodes at Vestry meeting
ζ Lydgate's misery. Rosamond's repulsion
η Mrs Bulstrode

(34)

Dorothea enters. Their confusion. Will hurriedly departs. Rosamond shivering. Dorothea repressing her anguish, carries out her intended admonition, & quits Rosamond.

Scene between Will & Dorothea[19]

Part VII.

1. Lydgate's affairs
2. Fred & Mary
3. Bulstrode's terrors & wish to get rid of the hospital.*
4. Lydgate sounds him. He is deaf. Raffles' illness & death. Loan to Lydgate.
5. Middlemarch suspicious &
6. Lydgate's misery.
7. [Outpouring to Dorothea.][20] Part VIII

* Action of Caleb Garth

(35)[21]

Lydgate goes to the Billiard room at G.D.
   (letter comes from Sir Godwin)
Fred Vincy is in the Billiard room
Mr Farebrother sends up for him
Walks with Fred to St Botolph's Parsonage & admonishes him that if he is not to lose Mary he must be careful.
Raffles having again been to Middlemarch—(seen by Lydgate in the billiard room) Bulstrode is meditating removal from Middlemarch going somewhere where he will have a less marked position & suffer less from the visits of Raffles. Is engaged in transferring his bank, & arranging the rest of his property for management without his personal presence. Is seeing Caleb Garth on this subject.
Hence Caleb is going to Stone Court on business. Overtakes Raffles who is ill
takes him up in his gig. Raffles tells Caleb everything about Bulstrode.
(Raffles has also told Bambridge)

Quarry II

(36)

1   That Raffles should tell the whole story of Bulstrode to Caleb Garth; that Caleb should remain silent on the subject even to his wife.
That Raffles should tell Bulstrode how Caleb knew all—but no one else than Caleb.
That Bulstrode sounds Caleb, who tells him his reasons for never disclosing
Caleb calls on Bulstrode tells him that Raffles is at Stone Court & in need of a doctor. Also declines to act further for Bulstrode.
Bulstrode calls in Lydgate.
Gives orders to the woman who sits up with Raffles, to administer opium & alcohol
Gives Lydgate the thousand pounds
Mr Farebrother, not knowing comes with help.
[Lydgate's anguish. Rosamond's repulsion] VIII.
Scene of outburst at a Vestry meeting in which Mr Hawley tells Bulstrode that he is known.
[Lydgate pours out to Dorothea about his misery, & she comforts him. VIII]

(37)
Conclusion of Part VII.

The discussion at Dollop's a type of what was going on in all Middlemarch circles.
The fact of his betrayal bursts upon Bulstrode at a Vestry meeting:
Returns home finds Mrs. Bulstrode partly informed: on Lydgate
   The news reaches Lowick & Freshitt
   Curtain follows on Dorothea's arrival

Query: connexion of Will's return[22]

(38)
Course of Part VII.

1. Mr Farebrother makes advances to Lydgate—refused.
2. Lydgate trying to get rid of his house: Rosd. thwarts him
3. Difficulties increase   Sir Godwin's letter comes
4. Lydgate goes to the billiard room. Fred Vincy is there: Mr Farebrother comes to fetch him.
5. Fred Vincy & he walk together
6. Lydgate begins to think of applying to Bulstrode. Bulstrode's efforts to free himself & wish to quit Middlemarch—business with Caleb Garth.
7. Lydgate sounds Bulstrode
8. Caleb Garth picks up Raffles. Takes him to Stone Court. Raffles tells him the secrets
9. Caleb calls on Bulstrode, who tells him Raffles is there & declines further transactions. Bulstrode suspects the reasons. Caleb reassures him as to secrecy. Execution in Lydgate's house
10. Bulstrode having called in Lydgate, neglects his orders, & causes Raffles to take alcohol etc.
11. Bulstrode calls on Lydgate & gives him £1000 or £500 (?)
12. Lydgate out of his difficulties. Scandal. Outburst of Mr Hawley against Bulstrode

(39)
Conditions
———
———

Return of Will Ladislaw: reasons for his return. Time at which it happens.
What becomes of Bulstrode's arrangements as to property, especially Stone Court?
   How Fred & Mary get married.
About Dorothea's money, over & above her own 700 a year.
Times
The death of Raffles about 21st. March

Quarry II

Bambridge's return 26th.
Meeting on Sanitary Reform, April 10th.
Return of Will Ladislaw

(40)

Part VIII

1 Dorothea & Lydgate
2 Dorothea goes to deliver a letter at Lydgate's
   Finds Will Ladislaw there. Suspicions confirmed by their emotion.

---

1 Reasons why Dorothea does not immediately have her interview with Lydgate.
3 Mrs Bulstrode made aware of the Facts about her husband.
   [Their final arrangements. Fred Vincy]
   Lydgate's misery [*written in above:* 2] & gloom.) Rosamond's repulsion.
   Will Ladislaw's arrival & its causes
3 Lydgate's outpouring to Dorothea. She takes the money to free him, & finds Will Ladislaw with Dorothea.[23] She goes away with the impression that they are lovers. Her emotions of jealousy: making her more distinctly aware of her love.
Her struggle to overcome her selfish feeling. She goes again to R.
Will's outburst to Rosamond after Dorothea is gone away: cutting to the quick.
When Dorothea comes again to Rosamond with love, Rosamond is wrought upon to tell her that Will loves Dorothea alone.

(41)

Dorothea's motive in going to Rosamond.

(42)[24]

Part VIII

1 Dorothea wants to help Lydgate & is checked
2 Lydgate's first anguish under the sense of his position
3 Mrs Bulstrode learns her sorrow

4   Rosamond's behavior & Lydgate's towards her
5   Lydgate tells Dorothea
6   Dorothea goes to see Rosamond & take (the £1000) money for Lydgate. Finds Will with Rosamond.
7   Will's outburst of bitterness against R.
8   Dorothea's anguish & struggles. She goes to Rosamond again who tells her about Will's truth.
9   Will's interview with Dorothea: Reconciliation
10 The Garths & Fred Vincy.
11 Dorothea tells her uncle & the Chettams that she is going to marry Will
12 Mr Brooke will be father at the wedding but as a corrective proposes to cut off the entail

          Finale

NOTES TO QUARRY TWO

(Notebook reversed)

[1] Miscellaneous dates, probably from the *Annual Register*.

[2] *Annual Register* probably used here also, but the data were available in many books. The author's statements add details.

[3] Page 2 is the verso of page 1. The right-hand pages are ordinarily numbered with odd numbers, the left with even; but occasionally a page is left blank and this rule is upset, e.g., page 11 is the verso of 10, and page 27 is a verso.

[4] The "letter on Hospitals" was written by Mrs. Richard Congreve, whose father, Dr. Bury, had attended Robert Evans in his last illness.

[5] Votes of the directors of the Middlemarch Infirmary cast in the choice of a chaplain.

[6] Many situations in the novel are timed to correspond with stages of the First Reform Bill; here the author gives her own timetable for important happenings in her story.

[7] Page 5 begins the listing of chapters with titles. Note that chapters 11 and 12, here listed in Part I, are transferred to Part II. The lack of paging here suggests the author's indecision about the proper place for these chapters.

[8] Note the changed wording of the chapter headings. The paging for these chapters, omitted on page 5, is given here.

[9] The difficulty of weaving in the Fred Vincy strands is seen on pages 6, 7, and 8 of *Quarry II*. The chapters listed as 19–21 were first included in Part II, but finally formed the opening chapters of Part III, numbered 22, 23, and 24. The original chapter 20 of Part II (see *Quarry II*, p. 6) is split into two chapters, 20 and 21. The original 21 becomes 22 and concludes Part II.

[10] Page 7, the verso of page 6, is a fair copy of page 8. The Vincy material is here logically and naturally interwoven with the Dorothea-Casaubon strand.

[11] Page 8 shows the process of working out the structure of Part III. Compare with page 7. "Dorothea Married," the original title of III, was crossed out and "Waiting for Death" substituted.

[12] The heading "Motives" covers a variety of details dealing with plot and characterization.

[13] The first rough estimate of the number of pages in Part IV, "pp. 150–170," is crossed out and "pp. 164" substituted.

[14] Here the "Motives (in general)" is followed by a further elaboration of Part V, previously dealt with chapter by chapter on page 12.

[15] The first item has already been listed on page 10 as "Mr Casaubon in prospect of death." The numbers to the left of the items are correct; the others are crossed. Note that with the renumbering of what was to have been the first chapter of Part V (originally 42, here 43) the chapters in the *Quarry* now correspond to those in the published text.

[16] On page 25 the important events of the Reform Bill period are narrated rather than merely listed. The probable source, again, is the *Annual Register*.

[17] See note 3.

[18] Page 29 works out in much greater detail the material outlined and then put into narrative form on pages 26 and 28.

[19] The first four lines on page 34 continue the "Sketch" on page 32. The seven items below deal with Part VII.

[20] The author began here to use square brackets as well as parentheses.

[21] Pages 35 and 36 deal with the complications of Part VII.

[22] The "Query" which concludes page 37 emphasizes the author's difficulty in fitting in Will's comings and goings.

[23] One of George Eliot's rare slips occurs when she writes "Dorothea" for "Rosamond" in the eighth line from the bottom.

[24] The numbered, clear list of chapters in Part VIII given on page 42 should be compared with page 15.

In the MS notebook, *Quarry II* shows many crossings-out, vertical, horizontal, and oblique. It seems neither possible nor important to reproduce these in print.

Bibliography

The Annual Register, London, 1830, 1832.

British Medical Journal (London), Dec. 5, 1931, p. 1053; Jan. 2, 1932, p. 27; Jan. 30, 1932, p. 204; Mar. 26, 1932, p. 578.

Cross, J. W. *George Eliot's Life as Related in Her Letters and Journals* (Edinburgh and London, 1885).

Cushing, Harvey. *Life of Sir William Osler* (New York: Oxford University Press, 1925).

Eliot, George. *Middlemarch* (Edinburgh and London, 1885).

An Exposition of the State of the Medical Profession in the British Dominions (London, 1826).

Gerhard, W. W. "Reports of Cases Treated in the Medical Wards of the Pennsylvania Hospital. Part 1st. Typhus and Remittent Fevers," *American Journal of the Medical Sciences*, XV (Feb., 1835): 320.

Gerhard, W. W. "On the Typhus Fever Which Occurred at Philadelphia in the Spring and Summer of 1836," *American Journal of the Medical Sciences*, XIX (Feb., 1837): 289–322; XX (Aug., 1837): 289–322.

Haight, Gordon S. *George Eliot and John Chapman* (New Haven: Yale University Press, 1940).

Huxley, T. H. "Cell Theory," *British and Foreign Medical and Chirurgical Review*, XII (1853): 285–314.

Kitchel, Anna T. *George Lewes and George Eliot* (New York: John Day, 1933).

The London Lancet, 1829–1833.

Power, Sir D'Arcy. "Medicine in the British Isles," *Clio Medica* (New York: Hoeber, 1930).

Raspail, F. V. *Nouveau système de chimie organique fondé sur des nouvelles méthodes d'observation*, etc. (Bruxelles, 1839).

Renouard, V. P. *History of Medicine*, Eng. transl. (Cincinnati, 1856).

Rolleston, Sir H. D. *Sir Clifford Allbutt: A Memoir* (London: Macmillan, 1929).

Russell, J. R. *History and Heroes of the Art of Medicine* (London, 1861).

Sprigge, Sir Squire. *Thomas Wakley, His Life and Times* (London, 1897).

Ware, John, M.D. *Remarks on the History and Treatment of Delirium Tremens* (Boston, 1831) (reprinted from the *Transactions of the Massachusetts Medical Society*).

Watson, Sir Thomas. *Lectures on the Principles and Practice of Physic* (Philadelphia, 1844).

White, F. *Warwickshire* (London, 1850).

www.ingramcontent.com/pod-product-compliance
Lightning Source LLC
Chambersburg PA
CBHW021716230426
43668CB00008B/857